*f*P

Also by Dr. Stephen Nowicki, Jr., and Dr. Marshall Duke

Teaching Your Child the Language of Social Success
Helping the Child Who Doesn't Fit In
Abnormal Psychology: A New Look
The Experience of Being Different

Will I Ever Fit In?

The Breakthrough Program for Conquering Adult Dyssemia

Stephen Nowicki, Jr., Ph.D., and Marshall Duke, Ph.D.

The Free Press
New York London Toronto Sydney Singapore

*f*P

THE FREE PRESS
A Division of Simon & Schuster, Inc.
1230 Avenue of the Americas
New York, NY 10020

For information regarding special discounts for bulk purchases,
please contact Simon & Schuster Special Sales at 1-800-456-6798
or business@simonandschuster.com

Designed by Deirdre C. Amthor

Manufactured in the United States of America

10 9 8 7 6 5 4 3 2 1

Library of Congress Cataloging-in-Publication Data

Nowicki, Stephen.
Will I ever fit in?: the breakthrough program for conquering adult dyssemia/Stephen Nowicki, Jr., and Marshall Duke.
p. cm.
Includes bibliographical references and index.
1. Nonverbal communication. 2. Interpersonal communication. 3. Body language. 4. Communicative disorders—Patients—Rehabilitation. I. Duke, Marshall P. II. Title.

RC423 .N69 2002
616.85'5—dc21
2001055645
ISBN 0-7432-0259-7

To those who taught us about relationships–

our colleagues
our clients
our students
our friends
and, most of all, our families

Contents

Acknowledgments

Our deepest thanks to Daniel Goleman, Melissa Faye Greene, Gary Morris, Philip Rappaport, and Beth Haymaker—each initially, for different reasons; all, ultimately, for the same reason.

Introduction

If you are reading this book, our guess is that you are someone searching for answers as to why you aren't happier with yourself and the relationships you have with others. Like most people in this situation, you've probably thought about why things aren't better and tried one approach or another, but solutions have probably eluded you. We believe that this is such a common experience because for decades professionals and laypeople alike have been looking for answers in the wrong place. Many of you may have heard a variant of the story about the person seen one evening on a city sidewalk crawling around under a lamppost, looking desperately for something. When asked by a passerby what he was looking for, the man replies, "I dropped my good fountain pen." The passerby then asks where he lost it and the man says, "Over there near the alleyway." When the passerby inquires why he is looking under the lamppost, then, and not over near the alleyway, the man says, "The light is much better over here!"

We believe that, for decades, those of us interested in the mechanisms of human relationships have also been looking only where the light has seemed to be better—in the domain of what people say to each other and in the words that we use. What we have discovered, however, is that if we move to where the light has not been traditionally directed—to nonverbal as opposed to verbal communication—we come upon many of the answers that have eluded us for so long. In a nutshell, what we have found is this: Problems in human relationships depend far less upon problems in verbal communication than they depend upon problems in nonverbal communication. People with difficulties in nonverbal communication have an identifiable and correctable condition—we call it *dyssemia*—that has been at the heart of their relationship woes.

Dyssemia is a term that we, the authors, coined in 1992 to refer to any significant difficulty in understanding or sending nonverbal information. The word, pronounced. "dis-SEM-ee-uh," is derived from the Greek "dys" for difficulty and "semes" for signs. It quite literally means a difficulty in using nonverbal signs or cues, and lies at one extreme of a dimension reflecting this skill. At the other extreme is *eusemia* (u-SEM-ee-uh), excellence in the ability to use nonverbal cues to establish and maintain successful and productive social and vocational relationships. As with most dimensions, most people will fall somewhere between the two extremes. However, if you or someone you know is more toward the dyssemic side of things, you (or they) are likely to be experiencing relational problems that you have not been able to understand. This is a book about identifying and overcoming dyssemia, the relationship-busting condition involving nonverbal communication errors that may be at the core of what's bothering you, just as it was for two people to whom we'd like to introduce you to right now.

Kyle

The business day had started with a rush. Mondays were always difficult in the office—so much to do, so little time to do it in. Rosita and Ruth were working on a project for improving sales of a new computer software program that their company had recently introduced. Their presentation had to be finished by noon. They were huddled close together just inside Rosita's office, looking at one of their project designs and talking in hushed tones. As they talked, something made them uneasy. They looked up and there was Kyle, one of their coworkers, standing close to them and staring at their plans. "How about those Cubs?" he said. Both Rosita and Ruth smiled curtly, said "Great" as they moved a few steps away from Kyle, and went back to looking at their drawings. Undaunted, Kyle moved closer to them and said, "You know, I think they ought to do away with interleague play. It really spoils the tradition of the game, doesn't it?" Rosita said, "Yes it probably does," then turned to Ruth and said, "Ruth, we need to go to your office to pick up the other project notes." With that, the two women stepped around Kyle and left him standing there staring after them.

Everybody knows somebody like Kyle. People like him populate offices, sales meetings, teacher lounges, church halls, bars, and anywhere else where people congregate. He's like the guy parodied on *Saturday Night Live* some years ago, who comments on and greets everyone going to the copying machine, saying something like, "Hello to the Big Ronski, the Ronator, going to copy something now, the Ronster is." Kyle, like this character, seems unaware of the negative effect he has on others. He cannot read others' cues accurately. The result is that regardless of who you are or where you are, whenever you see Kyle coming, you go the other way. You may even feel bad about avoiding Kyle; he seems nice enough, but for some reason being around him is just plain uncomfortable. He tries to fit in, but he just doesn't make it.

Even if we fill in the details of Kyle's background, it doesn't give us much of a clue as to why he is so difficult to be with. He was born and raised in a middle-sized midwestern city and attended college not very far from home. He has one sister, three years older, who is married and teaches fourth grade. Kyle is about six feet tall and weighs around 175 pounds. He dresses modestly and traditionally. Although Kyle is not movie-star handsome, his fair complexion and blond hair initially get him more than the usual amount of attention from the opposite sex. He has varied interests ranging from reading about the Civil War to skiing with the local ski club. At college he majored in engineering, played intramural sports, (especially softball), and dated a number of women—none for very long. After graduating with a B average, Kyle returned home to live with his parents while he looked for a job in the engineering field. His job-hunting was successful and he now works in the project office of a large company and is an avid baseball fan, with as absolute passion for the Chicago Cubs.

In many ways Kyle could be described as the typical all-American guy, but the truth is that he is not a happy man. Although he lives in an adequately furnished loft apartment, shares season tickets for the Cubs with three others, and is making a decent living, Kyle doesn't really have a close friend or, sadly, even many acquaintances. His season ticket plan gives him two tickets, but he often has difficulty finding anyone to go with him. Too many times Kyle ends up sitting next to a stranger who bought his extra ticket from him at the gate on game day. On the dating front, things are not much better. Kyle goes to clubs and nearly always manages to get women to go out with him once or twice, but rarely a third time.

The more he thinks about the way his life is, the more Kyle doesn't get it. Why does he have such a difficult time with people? He really wants desperately to have friends and to get married. He loves children and thinks he would make a good father. However, with the way things are going, he wonders if he'll ever have a close friend or find a woman who will make his dream of having a family come true. He knows something is wrong with his relationships and he believes the blame is his. He feels he must be doing something wrong, but is at a loss as to what it is.

We would call Kyle a *receptive dyssemic:* He has trouble reading the nonverbal cues of others. By nonverbal signs we mean all human responses that are not words (either spoken or written) but convey meaning, especially emotional meaning. Nonverbal behaviors include facial expressions, tone and inflection of voice (paralanguage), body movements and postures (sometimes called kinesics), gestures and touching, use of personal space (proxemics), and rhythm and use of time (chronemics). As mentioned, at the opposite end of the continuum from dyssemia is what we have called *eusemia,* or the ability to use nonverbal cues well.

In Kyle's interaction with Rosita and Ruth, for example, he misread cues in their facial expressions and ignored their personal space and postural cues, which indicated by their proximity to one another that they were involved in something that they'd prefer not to have interrupted. Kyle also didn't pick up on the tone of Rosita's voice, which communicated "Leave us alone, we're busy." Unfortunately, because of the underlying nature of nonverbal communication, Kyle didn't know that he was making these mistakes—he just thought he was being nice. When Rosita and Ruth left so abruptly, it reminded him of countless other times when people just went away for no reason he could understand. For their part, Rosita and Ruth were more aware of feeling uncomfortable around Kyle than of the actual reasons for their discomfort. As usually is the case with people on the receiving end of nonverbal mistakes, even if they knew what Kyle was doing to make them uncomfortable, they probably would not tell him because it would be considered "rude."

Amy

By contrast, Amy is an *expressive dyssemic.* Like the Kyles of this world you've also probably met people like Amy. Without conscious intent, and like all of us, this forty two-year-old woman sends myriad nonverbal cues about how she is feeling in her facial expressions, tone of voice, and postures. Unlike most other people, however, Amy's nonverbal cues do not reflect her true emotions. When most of us misrepresent our inner feelings nonverbally, we are fully aware of what we are doing, but Amy's way of communicating is different from simply "masking" how she truly feels in order to be polite or save someone's feelings. When one is not aware that one is, as one of our clients once said, "Advertising apples, but only selling oranges," misunderstanding, confusion, anxiety, and social and vocational problems can ensue. The potential consequences of communicating like Amy does are reflected in an incident that took place in the gift shop where she worked.

The Gift Shop

Joyce and Donna were making a tour of the small shops and boutiques in the newly renovated downtown part of the city. They were excited to see how an area that was once slums had been transformed into inviting shops and restaurants, and were thoroughly enjoying their day out and all the friendly shopkeepers and clerks they had met. Joyce wanted to try one more shop before going home, and Donna agreed. As luck would have it, it was the shop where Amy worked. Amy met them with words of greeting when they entered and told them to look around as much as they liked. The shop was beautifully renovated and stocked with wonderful antiques and memorabilia. However, as they walked about and examined the merchandise, Joyce and

Donna began to feel ill at ease. They could not shake the feeling that, for some reason, the store clerk was upset with them. Her words had been welcoming but somehow they didn't feel welcomed. The shop was attractive, but so were a dozen others where they felt much more comfortable than they did here. Within moments they left, without buying anything.

Although none of the participants was aware of it, what had made Joyce and Donna so uncomfortable was Amy's facial expression. Amy, who was feeling just fine, had a facial expression that was communicating that she was angry and upset. Amy suffers from an expressive dyssemia that is manifested in a "negative resting face." Our resting facial expression is the one that is shown when our thoughts and feelings are in neutral, when our face is just "hanging out." In Amy's case her resting face was unknowingly convincing others that she was upset when in fact she wasn't feeling that way. It was this expressive dyssemia that drove Joyce and Donna from the store, even though neither they nor Amy was aware that her facial expression was the cause of their flight.

Although she has been employed on and off for nearly all of her adult life, Amy's work situations have always been troubled. As Joyce and Donna had done, people responded to the unpleasant atmosphere created by her negative resting facial expressions by avoiding her. It probably didn't help matters that Amy naturally stood with her arms folded and had a "hard" tone of voice. Overall, regardless of the words she spoke and how she actually was feeling, Amy gave an impression of being a very angry person. For Amy's part, she could not understand why people were so negative and rejecting of her. To her way of thinking, she always tried to be nice and say the right things, but people just didn't seem to appreciate her and to reciprocate her kind words. This is because of the basic fact that whenever there is a difference between the verbal and nonverbal messages we send, others will most often believe and respond to the nonverbal one.

Perhaps an example of what we mean would be helpful here.

Comedian Jerry Seinfeld had a long-running show that is now in syndication. Much of this successful comedian's humor derives from his knowledge of nonverbal communication. In one of his shows he expertly and humorously showed how much more attention we pay to nonverbal than to verbal messages. In this show, George, one of the ongoing characters, inadvertently squirted grapefruit juice in his eye while eating breakfast. As a result, for the rest of the day George was forced to blink his eye in response to the irritation. This blink looked very much like a wink. For the next eight hours George was unknowingly winking at those with whom he interacted. In one scene, George's top boss comes to his office to ask George's opinion about his immediate supervisor and the kind of job George thinks he is doing. George lauds his immediate supervisor with his words, but at the end of his endorsement speech his eye is bothering him, so he winks. The top boss, seeing this, responds by saying, "Oh, I understand. You don't have to say another word." What had happened was that the simple wink of an eye had changed the entire meaning of George's words from support to criticism.

Like George, Amy was unwittingly sending signals she didn't intend, both in the workplace and in her personal relationships. A very attractive dark-haired woman, Amy had always been able to get men's attention, but had not been able to sustain a relationship for any substantial length of time—each of her three engagements ended shortly in a breakup. Amy believes that the reason for her failures with men is that they are basically shallow and thoughtless.

Amy, like Kyle, is unhappy and knows that something is very wrong in her life. Similar to Kyle, Amy is unaware that she is the cause of many of her interpersonal troubles. However, unlike Kyle, who blames himself for his relationship problems and, as a result, is depressed and anxious about his perceived shortcomings, Amy does not see herself playing any part, even innocently, in her problems. Rather, she blames her difficulties on others and is angry at them for making her life so unpleasant. Amy deplores what she perceives as the insensitivity of others, who thwart her every attempt to connect with them. This is especially true in her feelings about men. Amy sees men as just using her for sex and then moving on to the next "victim." Because of her belief that others are to blame for her relationship difficulties, she enters relationships with a skeptical attitude and an expectancy that they will fail. Not surprisingly, her expressive dyssemia coupled with her negative expectancies ensures that Amy's predictions of failure are usually correct.

Kyle and Amy are two of what we believe is a countless number of individuals who have problems with their relationships because they are dyssemic. Based on dozens of studies with literally thousands of individuals of all ages, we now know, with confidence, that the more extensive dyssemias are, the more damage they can have on our relationships. Dyssemic individuals suffer from feelings of lower self-esteem and self-worth, and greater social anxiety and loneliness. They have fewer friends and experience unpleasant social outcomes such as rejection by peers and greater marital discord and dissatisfaction. Dyssemias can occur in people at all levels of intelligence and socioeconomic standings. Intelligence as measured by traditional IQ tests is no protection against the occurrence of dyssemia and its potentially negative consequences.

How We First Learned about Dyssemias and Their Negative Whallop

We'll begin by taking you back into the late 1960s and early 1970s. Imagine looking at the world through the eyes of two young professors trying to figure out why some people wind up unhappy and lost while many of their age-mates seem to sail along basically content with their lot in life. Remember, this was decades before Dan Goleman's groundbreaking book *Emotional Intelligence,* which was published in 1995.

Though the significance of nonverbal processing skills seems so obvious today, that wasn't always the case. When we first began, the study of nonverbal behavior was seen as a pop-psychology fad that would come and go and occasionally find its way into a magazine article, most often under the term "body language." As our knowledge of nonverbal behavior increased we soon became convinced that it was not just another pop fad, but was actually a fundamentally important way that people communicated and linked up with one another. How we came to that conclusion originated in our experiences with two widely divergent but troubled groups of people: severely disturbed children and adolescents and adult clients in psychotherapy.

Severely Disturbed Children and Adolescents

The children and adolescents we saw suffered from a variety of severe disorders ranging from schizophrenia to depression intense enough to cause suicide attempts. They were receiving treatment in what were called "psychoeducational centers." There are twenty-six such centers sprinkled across the cities and towns of Georgia, each providing treatment to youngsters who otherwise would have to be hospitalized. We were privileged to be consultants at several of these fine centers.

Jared

Although we enjoyed working with all of the children, Jared, a tall, gawky fourteen-year-old who was diagnosed with a variety of severe disorders, was one of our favorites, winning our hearts with his persistence and determination to improve himself. During one week in the fall, the staff was attempting to teach Jared some much-needed social skills, and wanted him to practice on visitors. Steve happened to be on a consulting visit to the center at this time, so he became one of Jared's "volunteers." As Steve stood in the entry hall to the center, Jared slowly walked up to him, stopped about an inch in front of his nose, and said, "Good morning, Dr. Nowicki. How are you?" Jared had been taught to use the socially correct words to greet someone, but unfortunately not the socially acceptable nonverbal behaviors regarding use of space. When Steve moved back to provide the correct distance for such a conversation, Jared moved forward again. The next time Steve moved back he put his arm out and said to Jared, "This is about how far you want to stand when saying hello to someone; you need to be able to put your arm out. That is about how far away you should stand." With this cue, Jared once again said the words of greeting but this time at the correct interpersonal distance to make a socially appropriate communication.

Jared was not the only child we met with these kinds of nonverbal difficulties; in fact, it was clear that almost all the children at the center had glaring multiple nonverbal processing handicaps. Because the nonverbal deficits were so obvious and easily seen, they caught and held our attention. It became obvious to us that children such as Jared needed to be taught directly and concretely the correct ways of using nonverbal behavioral cues. Without such direct teaching, Jared and his psychoeducational center peers would continue to make the kind of nonverbal mistakes that would keep them ostracized from others, no matter how much progress they made in other areas of their treatment.

Psychotherapy Clients

On the whole, psychotherapy clients are usually brighter and less disturbed than psychoeducational center children, but we soon found out that dyssemias interfered with their social adjustment and happiness as well. Take Dorothy, for example.

Learning about Dyssemia: Dorothy

Dorothy was a successful thirty-two-year-old businesswoman. Fitness training, including workouts in the weight room, had produced a healthy, strong woman who was rightfully very proud of her size-four figure. At the time she decided to begin psychotherapy, personal problems she had previously experienced with men were popping up again in her relationship with Ted, a man she really liked. She wanted their relationship to be successful and decided therapy might be a way to make that happen. In therapy, she reported that Ted often complained that he never knew what she was really feeling, that she would say everything was fine but then blow a gasket a short time later. Dorothy volunteered that this was not the first time a man had voiced this criticism of her, but she didn't exactly know what it meant. She was not to remain in the dark for long.

At one particular session, Dorothy came in a few minutes late and sat down. While her fashionable gray double-breasted business suit, nicely styled hair, and near-perfect makeup said she had her act together, her nonverbal behavior communicated something quite different. Her face was flushed, her fists were clenched; she held her head in a stiff and rigid position and sat with her arms folded across her chest. Marshall thought he was on pretty solid ground when he asked her why she was so angry. She looked at him with great surprise and said, "Angry? I'm not angry. Sure, it's been a trying day, but I don't think I'm angry." When Marshall pointed out all of the nonverbal indicators of anger she flushed even more deeply. With more feedback from Marshall about how her head and neck posture, clenched fists, and flushed skin communicated her anger, Dorothy began to acknowledge that she was indeed angry as hell. Dorothy's realization that her true feelings were being communicated nonverbally outside of her awareness marked a significant turning point in her psychotherapy. She began to understand why Ted might be confused about how she was feeling, because the truth of the matter was, so was she. Dorothy was but one of literally hundreds of clients we have seen whose problems could be traced back to the fact that they were unaware of communicating one message with their words and another, sometimes opposite in meaning, with their nonverbal behavior.

The Secret Uncovered: Why Dyssemias Wreak Havoc on Relationships

We are indebted to our past clients, both children and adults, for helping to steer us toward what was significant in their communications with us. Through their insights, they sensitized us to the fact that every time they spoke to us, in reality, they were sending us two messages—one verbal and the other nonverbal—and that both were important, though sometimes in different ways. As later research was to confirm, we saw a consistent presence of nonverbal difficulties in individuals with personal and social adjustment problems. Nonverbal errors were important, but the question kept nagging at us: Why were they so important? What was it about nonverbal communication that made it so crucial to relationships?

First of all, it is clear to us that nonverbal communication is *further removed from awareness than verbal language.* In fact, most of the time we forget that nonverbal communication is going on at all. Think about it! Unless we direct your attention to, and make you aware of, the way you are sitting while reading this page, the possible expression you may have on your face, and how far away you may be sitting from other people, you will be largely oblivious to these and other nonverbal behaviors that are going on in and around you. We know this because even though we have studied the area of nonverbal communication for nearly thirty years, the truth is that most of the time we are just like you: unaware of our own or others' nonverbal messages. While lecturing, both of us have experienced the shock of momentarily becoming aware of our waving hands and arms, only in the next instant to completely forget about our wild gesturing as we go on to make another point.

Because we usually are not aware of the constant ebb and flow of nonverbal communication going on around us, the implication is that we also are not aware of how good or bad we are at processing this kind of information. Unfortunately, it is very hard to determine how adept we really are. Unlike with verbal ability, where our basic skills are assessed starting in the early school grades, we take no standardized tests and receive no formal feedback about our strengths and weaknesses in nonverbal language usage. We are largely in the dark about our nonverbal abilities. Even when people are aware of our nonverbal behavior, they will resist telling us if we have problems in this area. This is unfortunate because while most of us have an accurate sense of how strong our verbal skills are, results from our studies show that there is little relation between how adept we think we are nonverbally and how skilled we actually are. In fact, recent research has shown that, if anything, most people overestimate their nonverbal skill.

Not only are we less aware of what we are communicating nonverbally than we are of the words we are speaking, but our nonverbal communications are also *more continuous.* This second, seemingly simple, unique nonverbal characteristic has tremendous implications for interpersonal interactions. Consider this: We can stop communicating with words any time we want; we can stop talking or writing at will; but we would find it much more difficult, if not impossible, to stop communicating nonverbally. Our facial expressions, postures, gestures, and other nonverbal behaviors continue to send emotional messages whether we want them to or not. Likewise, we cannot help but be affected by the nonverbal behaviors of others. As Paul Watzlawick, one of the originators of research on verbal and nonverbal communication in psychotherapy, put it very clearly, "You cannot *not* communicate nonverbally!"

Our third difference has to do with what happens to others when we make a verbal or a nonverbal communication mistake. We all have made verbal mistakes ranging from misspelling words to using the wrong grammar. Often the effect of this is to make others conclude that the speaker or writer is uneducated or perhaps not very intelligent. In addition, sometimes these verbal grammatical miscues can be humorous. The following verbal grammatical mistakes were taken from actual church bulletins.

- Don't let worry kill you, let the church help
- For those of you who have children and don't know it, we have a nursery downstairs.
- This afternoon there will be a meeting in the south and north ends of the church. Children will be baptized at both ends.
- Thursday at 5:00 P.M. there will be a meeting of the Little Mothers Club. All wishing to become a Little Mother, please see the minister in his study.

- This being Easter Sunday, we will ask Mrs. Lewis to come forward and lay an egg on the altar.
- The ladies of the church have cast off clothing of every kind and they may be seen in the church basement Friday.
- At the evening service tonight, the sermon topic will be "What is Hell?" Come early and listen to our choir practice.

The story is much different when you break equivalent nonverbal "grammatical" rules. Let us give you an example of what we mean.

Steve was convinced by his wife to go and see the latest art film. She lauded everything about the film, especially the directing and the script. Although not a fan of art films, Steve relented and drove down to the movie theater to take in the feature. After buying popcorn and a Coke, he took a seat. He noticed that there were no more than eight people in a theater that could seat three hundred, but that was comparable to other art film crowds he had been a part of in the past. He relaxed and waited for the movie to begin. After a few moments, however, he noticed out of the corner of his eye that someone else had entered the theater. The new moviegoer looked around and began to walk slowly down the aisle. The stranger stopped at the row where Steve was sitting and began moving again until stopping at the seat right next to Steve and sitting down. So there they sat, two strangers sitting side-by-side in a movie theater with 291 other empty seats. Steve instantly felt uncomfortable and even a little bit frightened by this action. Before another minute had passed he got up, mumbling something about needing to go to the rest room before the movie began, but in reality he left the theater, got in his car, and drove home.

• • •

We think you also would have reacted in the way Steve did if a stranger came and sat down next to you in a movie theater where there were hundreds of other empty seats. The question is, why would you feel so threatened? The answer is a simple one: The stranger was breaking a nonverbal rule of personal space usage. You just do not sit next to someone you do not know in a movie theater where there are hundreds of other empty seats available! In chapter 2 we'll show you how this rule can be expanded and applied to every empty space you have to share with others. The simple but profound truth is that when we break nonverbal rules of communication, rather than having a negative intellectual effect (as happens most often in the case of verbal communication errors), we usually will have a negative *emotional* impact. Our nonverbal errors tend to make others feel uncomfortable, and sometimes even anxious or frightened.

Sociologist Thomas Scheff was interested in the sorts of characteristics that cause us to identify other people's behavior as troubling. In the mildest instance, he was interested in behaviors that are unsettling or bothersome; in the most extreme cases, he was interested in what we label as mental illness. He proposed that one thing all unsettling interpersonal behaviors have in common is that they represent violations of what he termed "residual rules," which are not noticed until they are broken. They are residual because they would be the "rules" left over after we hypothetically write down all of the official and formal rules of society that are codified by our systems of etiquette and justice. Examples of residual rules are plentiful because their number is nearly infinite. One rule, for instance, says that when we are sitting in a room involved in almost any activity, we do not touch anyone else. We know that this is a rule, because if we break it, we ask forgiveness from those we've offended by saying, "Oh I am so sorry, pardon me!"

In a proper setting, the violation of residual rules can be the stuff of comedy, and we will look more closely at this possibility later. However, it is anything but funny when someone sits next to us in an empty theater, stands too close when conversing, or touches us when and where we do not want them to. The fact is that the "grammar" of nonverbal language is to be found in the residual rules that Scheff identified. Residual rules govern the use of nonverbal language in the same way that grammar rules govern the use of verbal language. The big difference is that violation of a residual rule causes other people to be uncomfortable around us and, depending upon the severity of our violation, may lead to them avoiding or rejecting us outright.

The Dyssemic Core

So what do the three unique characteristics of nonverbal communication have to do with our main interest, relationships? Just about everything! In fact, these three characteristics form what we have come to call the "dyssemic core," a particular set of circumstances that can put our relationship success at risk. Why? Because when we make nonverbal mistakes we have a *negative emotional impact* on others, we have it *continuously*, and we *will not even be aware* that we are making the mistakes. We may be aware of the fact that things are not going well interpersonally, but like Kyle and Amy, we probably will not be aware that it is our very own nonverbal mistakes that are the source and cause of our personal and social difficulties. It is an elegant trap that dyssemics unknowingly and innocently set for themselves. Their lack of awareness prevents them from making the connection between the negative reactions of others and the source of this social rejection, their own nonverbal errors.

Dyssemics unknowingly "pull" negative reactions from others. Unlike in the case of a learning-disabled person whose teachers and parents are aware of his or her word-related difficulties and are eager to offer help, dyssemics, as well as those with whom they interact, are unaware of what dyssemics are unwittingly doing to sabotage their own attempts to relate to others. Even at those times when others are aware of the nonverbal mistakes dyssemics are making, few would feel comfortable enough to confront such people directly, because of the fear of appearing rude and hurting the person's feelings. How many of us know someone who stands too close when he or she talks? Dresses poorly or wears too much perfume or aftershave? Touches us too often or inappropriately during conversation? Talks in boring monotone or punctuates her words with "ahhs" and "umms"? How often have you told the person in these instances that what they were doing was annoying? Not often, we bet—and therein lies a major roadblock to the awareness and new learning that dyssemic individuals so dearly need in order to make their attempts at relating to others more successful.

What Kinds of Dyssemia Are There?

At the beginning of the chapter we introduced two general kinds of dyssemias reflected by our descriptions of Kyle and Amy: *receptive* (difficulty reading cues of others accurately) or *expressive* (errors in sending nonverbal information correctly). Receptive and expressive dyssemias can occur within one or more of the various channels of nonverbal communication. What follows is a brief description of the types of nonverbal communication that will be expanded on in chapters 3, 4, and 5.

Rhythm represents the pace at which we do things. A fast pace can communicate urgency or impatience; a slow pace might indicate relaxation or even confusion, depending upon situational factors. However, rhythm also represents a basic way of living that actually varies from family to family, from region to region, and from country to country. At Emory University we constantly see the more rapid pace of northeastern students collide with the more languid rhythm of those from the South. Unfortunately, differences in pace are often misconstrued as personality characteristics. For example, we have heard more fast-paced northern students be described as "rude" by southerners, while those from the South are sometimes described as "slow" by northerners. We've noticed that because of their basic rhythm of speech and movement (denoting what area of the country they may be from), we can have an instant like or dislike for strangers we meet at conferences and workshops.

The use of space, or what experts call *proxemics,* involves how close or how far we stand from people while interacting with them. We can express feelings of caring for others by getting close to them, and, conversely, we can reduce the likelihood of a relationship's developing by keeping our distance. The rules for space usage are very complex and important. Consider our earlier description of Steve in the empty movie theater, or of Kyle standing too close when talking to Rosita and Ruth.

Facial expressions are probably the most obvious form of nonverbal behavior. In their daily discourse, people must be able to produce facial expressions that are clear and accurate representations of their internal states or, perhaps even more important, be able to mask their internal states when it is socially appropriate to do so. Remember Amy? Her facial expressions were very much involved in the unsatisfactory social interactions she experienced. Unknown to her, her facial expression was not reflecting what she was feeling, but instead was communicating something negative and off-putting. More often, masking is used to put on a "happy face" to cover up negative feelings.

Voice tone, loudness, and pace of actual words are all part of *paralanguage.* It is not the actual words someone uses that alone produce the communicative impact, it is also the way the words are said. For example, think of the dozens of ways that the word "okay" may be used. This very simple utterance can be sent in such a way as to be positive, negative, neutral, loving, or even hateful. A challenge in paralanguage use is learning how the words used can be varied, when a particular tone is appropriate, and what, upon hearing the word used, another person is actually trying to communicate to us.

Gestures are important as the "batons" of interpersonal transactions. They regulate the flow of conversation and give emphasis to what is being said. They involve the hands and arms and vary considerably from culture to culture.

On the other hand, *postures* are unique because they function as the "long-distance" channel. That is, we can read and send information about feelings even when we are not near enough to hear voices or see faces. Thus, for example, teachers often tell us that they can determine the mood of their classroom simply by peering in the doorway and observing the way the students are sitting.

Style of dress, hair style, jewelry, and other decorations that carry meaning about us to others (and to ourselves) are referred to by experts as *fashion* or *objectics.* Unlike other nonverbal channels that tend to retain their same meanings over long periods of time, the meanings of objectics tend to shift with time. What communicates "I'm with it" one day can potentially communicate "I'm really out of it" the next.

Chronemics refers to the information about us that is communicated through our use of time. For example, a good way to ruin an important job interview is to arrive twenty minutes late. "Giving of our time" to our children is also a powerful way to show them that we care.

How Do People Become Dyssemic?

If you are someone who is dyssemic and is experiencing its detrimental effects in your relationships, you are probably wondering how you came to have this problem. Your first question probably is, "Was I born this way?" Our answer is, probably not. Some people may be born with a brain that does not take in or express nonverbal information correctly, but we believe that most newborns come with the necessary neurological wiring required to process nonverbal language cues. What we believe is that most of you are perfectly capable of learning nonverbal cues but are dyssemic because you haven't had a chance to learn how to communicate effectively nonverbally.

Think about the sources of dyssemia this way: Our research suggests that if we were to test one hundred people in the population, we would find that about ten of them had some form of dyssemia. We think that about one of the ten would be dyssemic because of some biological-neurological reason—perhaps he or she was born with this neurological shortcoming, or acquired it from some physical trauma like an auto accident or disease. Of the nine remaining dyssemics, we estimate that another one or two of them would have developed their nonverbal problems because they experienced some long-term psychological stress that interfered with the normal learning of nonverbal cues that takes place during childhood. Stressful events include contentious divorces, severe illnesses, abuse, and any other set of events that might make young children so emotionally upset that their learning of the connections between nonverbal cues and internal emotional states is interrupted. The remaining seven or eight of the ten dyssemic individuals would have nonverbal processing problems because they simply failed to learn the cues that they were perfectly capable of learning.

How could such a significant number of people fail to learn something so basic and important as associating nonverbal cues with internal states, something that most others do so easily? Our research shows that individuals become dyssemic because, unlike verbal language, which is *formally* and *directly* taught to children first by parents in the home and later by teachers in schools, nonverbal language is learned *indirectly* and *informally* by observing and imitating others' bahavior. To maximize their ability to pair nonverbal cues with internal emotional states, children need to watch others (most often parents) express important emotions at all levels of intensities. The reality, though, is that most families usually emphasize some emotions over others and express them more often at one level of intensity or another. Since there is no standardized testing of nonverbal skills in children, and nonverbal behavior takes place largely out of our awareness, dyssemias can develop without people being aware they have them.

About This Book: Helping the Kyles and Amys of This World

Okay, we have introduced you to the concept of dyssemia and have described some people who are dyssemic. Perhaps you saw bits of yourself in Kyle and Amy. Perhaps the nonverbal source of their relationship problems is the same as yours. Perhaps it may be found in some other areas of nonverbal communication. Your task is, with our help, to move from loneliness to belonging, from a feeling of helplessness in your interpersonal relationships to a sense of control, from apprehension in the process of meeting new people to a feeling of optimism and hope, from dyssemia and all of its emotional costs toward eusemia with all of its benefits.

In this first chapter we've attempted to help you understand what nonverbal communication is and the critical ways that lapses in it can undermine your attempts to connect with others. The rest of the book describes a three-step program to take you from dyssemia toward its positive counterpart, eusemia—the improved ability to use nonverbal communication effectively in your personal and vocational lives. In the first of these three steps we provide ways for you to determine if you have difficulties in understanding, expressing, or making sense out of nonverbal information. If it is determined that you do have nonverbal difficulties, then step two presents ways of preparing to deal with the specific kinds of dyssemia you may be experiencing. This preparation readies you for step three, in which we guide you through the tasks necessary to correct your nonverbal errors and become a more effective and successful person.

If all this sounds like something that might apply to you, we're eager to be of help. We're ready to move forward to step one and begin the task of determining if you are dyssemic. As Robert Frost once said, "You come, too."

Chapter 1

Are You Dyssemic?

It should be clear by now that being dyssemic can make life very difficult. But are *you* dyssemic? And might that dyssemia be contributing to your social and vocational interpersonal relationship problems? Because nonverbal communication operates mostly out of your awareness, you probably do not know what your nonverbal processing abilities are. Because the most obvious sign that you may be dyssemic is that you are having problems with relationships, we have developed a short test to give you some idea of whether or not you are having the kinds of difficulties that would be associated with being dyssemic. Make a copy of the self-assessment, Am I Dyssemic?, and follow the instructions for its completion. You will need to get someone to help you on the first part. Even though this may take time, we suggest you put this book aside and complete the scales before you read further.

Am I Dyssemic?

Part I: Questions About You

Ask someone whom you trust to complete the rating scale below. It may be a spouse, family member, or coworker, but it must be someone who has known you for some time and observed you in many different situations. This may be hard for you to do, but it is critical. Remember, most people who know dyssemics may be aware of many of the things they do wrong interpersonally, but for fear of hurting the dyssemic person's feelings, they simply will not say anything unless given permission. You must give permission to your helper for this scale to be effective. Just do it!

Never or very rarely	*Sometimes*	*Often*	*Always or very frequently*
1 point	*2 points*	*3 points*	*4 points*

_____ 1. Can come off as tactless or insensitive.
_____ 2. Appears not as intelligent as he or she is.
_____ 3. Seen by others as lacking in social maturity.
_____ 4. Seems to miss cues indicating danger or emotional upset in the physical and social environment.
_____ 5. Has difficulty understanding and following spoken or unspoken rules where groups or teams interact, especially in social interactions.
_____ 6. Seems generally to feel sad, anxious, bewildered, or isolated.
_____ 7. Persists in approaches to relationships even though they fail.
_____ 8. Seems unable to perceive any connections between his or her behavior and what happens.
_____ 9. Seems to have trouble making and keeping friends.
_____ 10. Dresses inappropriately for situations.

Total Points for Items 1 through 10:_____(Range: 10 to 40)

Part II: Questions for You

The next fifteen items are to be answered by you. Use the same rating system as above.

Never or very rarely	*Sometimes*	*Often*	*Always or very frequently*
1 point	*2 points*	*3 points*	*4 points*

_____ 11. I do not feel very good about myself.
_____ 12. I am often at a loss for how to begin a conversation with others.
_____ 13. I cannot explain why a particular relationship *did not* work out.
_____ 14. I cannot understand why a particular relationship *did* work out.
_____ 15. I don't know why others get angry at me.
_____ 16. I have trouble making small talk.
_____ 17. I do not succeed in getting a second or third date with someone I have met.
_____ 18. After spending several hours with someone, I find I do not know very much about him or her.
_____ 19. I feel very anxious when I am trying to meet or make a good impression on someone.
_____ 20. I feel sad and alone.
_____ 21. I feel confused and unsure about relationships with others.
_____ 22. I have been counseled by my employers about some aspect of my interpersonal behavior.
_____ 23. I have thought that an interaction with someone was very successful, only to find out later that it was a failure.
_____ 24. As a child, I was left out of games or rarely picked early when choosing sides.
_____ 25. As a child, I was not invited to many parties and other social activities.

Total Points for Items 11 through 25_____(Range: 15 to 60)
Total Points for Part I plus Part II:_____(Range: 25 to 100)

Okay, if you've completed the scales, let's examine your score.

As you can see, the lowest score possible is a 25 and the highest is 100. However, in this case, a score of 100 would not be the ideal it is in other tests. While there is not a formal cutoff score that we can give you, we can provide some general guidelines. First, the higher the score, the more likely it is that you may be dyssemic.

25 to 35: You are likely to get along pretty well with others and are unlikely to be dyssemic.
36 to 50: Very soft signs of dyssemia. There may be some areas in which you could develop your social skills further.
51 to 75: Any score in this range suggests a significant problem interpersonally and there is a good chance that what we suggest in this book may be very helpful to you.
76 to 100: Scores in this range suggest that what we have to offer in this book will be helpful, but may need to be supplemented by additional assessment and counseling from education and mental health professionals. (We have included in the appendix the names of some organizations from whom referrals may be obtained.)

There will be some people with low scores on the scale who can still benefit from practice in the language of relationships, and there will be some high-scorers who are content with the way they function and their level of social and vocational success. Psychological scales, like the people who develop them and the people who use them, are by nature not perfect. Don't let a number dictate to you; instead, let the number be one of the factors you consider in deciding if you might be dyssemic.

After the Questionnaire: Now What?

By completing the questionnaire you've given yourself an idea about whether or not you are dyssemic and if your lack of skill in nonverbal communication might be interfering with your attempts to connect with people. As we said, no single test should be the final word on whether you are dyssemic. That is why we want you to do a little more work in determining if you are dyssemic and having interpersonal difficulties as a result. To do this we must describe two common companions of dyssemia: anxiety and feelings of powerlessness.

Watch Out for Anxiety!

Because of the unique ways it interferes with your attempts to get along with others, anxiety is one of the major roadblocks to your being a happy and adjusted person. The most damaging aspect of anxiety in relationships is that it makes people pay more attention to it and what it is doing to them than to what it is doing to the others with whom they are interacting. When we are anxious, what we pay attention to is our anxiety.

One of the major causes of anxiety is nonverbal processing difficulty. When we notice that we are failing in our attempts to connect with others, our self-esteem is threatened. Because relationships are so complex and difficult, and are so often characterized by failure, they claim most of our awareness and we are almost always in danger of feeling anxious. Any interpersonal contact can result in failure that can potentially make us feel humiliation, shame, and, of course, anxiety because we have failed someone else as well as ourselves. Anxiety is a signal that results from others having rejected us interpersonally, and from the fear that they may do so again in the present or future.

Take a moment to complete the brief anxiety scale on the following page.

Measuring Your Anxiety

Please answer the following questions with either:

Not at all	*Sometimes*	*Often*
1 point	*2 points*	*3 points*

_____ 1. I worry about making errors.
_____ 2. I worry about embarrassing myself.
_____ 3. I am afraid much of the time.
_____ 4. I have trouble sleeping at night.
_____ 5. It is difficult for me to make up my mind about things.
_____ 6. I worry that I will fail in whatever I try.
_____ 7. I have trouble making decisions.
_____ 8. I get upset too easily.
_____ 9. I worry about things I did in the past.
_____ 10. I worry about the future.

Now add up your ratings on all items. Scores can range from 10 to 30. The higher your score, the more likely it is that anxiety will be interfering with your processing of interpersonal information.

Why Is Anxiety so Detrimental to Interpersonal Adjustment?

The answer to the question above is a pretty simple one. Anxiety essentially paralyzes our ability to learn. Step back from yourself a moment and think about how you think and feel when you are anxious. Don't you find it difficult if not impossible to pay attention to anything else going on around you? And if you are not paying attention to what is going on around you, how can you successfully process the constant flow of nonverbal information between you and others? Not surprisingly, when we are only paying attention to how anxious we are, it can affect our ability to read others' nonverbal cues accurately. A good example of what we mean took place between one of this book's authors, Steve, and his wife while he was working, ironically enough, on this very chapter.

Anxiety and Steve's Wife

Steve's wife just came in from working all day at her chaplain's job at the hospital. Along with the anxiety implicit in her job was the additional anxiety of feeling that Steve would be upset with her for working such long hours away from home. This was one of those moments. In truth, Steve was so involved in writing this book that he had lost track of time, so when he saw her he smiled widely and told her how glad he was to see her. Instead of picking up that his nonverbal and verbal messages were positive, her anxiety had altered her perception and led her to conclude that Steve was angry with her. Luckily, Steve was working on this chapter at the time and asked her to come over to the word processor and read what he had just finished writing about the potentially paralyzing effects of anxiety on the processing of interpersonal information. When she finished reading, they both had a good laugh about the coincidence, made some coffee, and sat down at the dining room table to talk about their respective days' experiences. However, the truth was that they had dodged an interpersonal bullet. Without the awareness of the potentially paralyzing effects of anxiety, it could have warped Steve's wife's perceptions and then Steve's own, and produced an unpleasant interaction. In turn, an unpleasant interaction could have generated more anxiety for both of them, further hampering their ability to read one another accurately and leading to even more difficult interactions in the future.

Has the above or something like it ever happened to you? Have you ever been so anxious that you completely misread the intentions of others or sent inappropriate nonverbal messages yourselves? Although dyssemia often does cause anxiety, it is also true that once the anxiety is present it can further disrupt the processing of nonverbal cues. In contrast to the kind of dyssemia that is a more permanent fixture—*trait dyssemia*—we call this temporary disruption *situational dyssemia.* In situational dyssemia, anxiety can make you dyssemic even if you normally are not. If you are already dyssemic, anxiety can worsen its impact.

Jeremy: Situational Dyssemia and the First Date

Jeremy was a basket case. For weeks he had wanted to ask Cherie out on a date, but every time he got around her his voice would stammer and he'd look at the ceiling instead of into her eyes. After these interactions with Cherie, Jeremy would go to the men's room at the office and berate himself for being so stupid. He would hit himself in the head with his hand as though his brain was out of kilter and a good firm slam would put the out-of-line parts back in order. Then he would look in the mirror tell himself to get control.

Jeremy practiced the simple sentences that he'd use to invite Cherie to the symphony. How hard could it be to say, "Hi, Cherie. Would you like to come with me to the symphony this Saturday? They're playing a Bach program and it should be great." Finally, on Tuesday morning, he screwed up all his courage and as he passed Cherie's desk he stopped and blurted out the sentences he had been practicing in secret. Cherie looked up at him with a surprised expression on her face and said, "Jeremy, how sweet of you. I'd love to go." Jeremy breathed a great sigh of relief and said, "Terrific, I'll pick you up at 7:30." After Jeremy had gone, Cherie turned to her officemate and said, "Can you believe it, Jeremy asked me to go to the symphony. From the way he'd been acting I thought he really didn't like me. What a surprise!"

• • •

Jeremy was lucky. Being a situational dyssemic did not lead to social disaster, but it very easily could have. Whether you are usually dyssemic or are made temporarily dyssemic for a time by anxiety, misreading or mis-sending nonverbal cues can worsen your interpersonal problems and that, in turn, can trigger even more anxiety. The keys to breaking this potentially vicious circle are to either reduce anxiety or increase awareness of nonverbal mistakes—or, in the best of all possible worlds, to do both.

When Anxiety Makes People Powerless

One of the most potentially devastating effects of prolonged anxiety is that it can begin to affect the basic way we look at our interpersonal world. Uncontrollable anxiety and relationship problems may lead us to believe that our own efforts don't have much to do with what occurs in our lives and that what happens to us is due more to outside factors like luck, fate, chance, or powerful others. How we view the connection between what we do and what happens to us is called our *locus of control.* Since the word *locus* means "place" or "location," this characteristic is most easily thought of as a belief about *where* the control is in our lives—inside of us or outside of us. Although the term isn't familiar to most people, it is the single most researched aspect of personality in the history of psychology. Part of the reason for its astounding popularity is because it is related to so many aspects of our lives. According to psychologist Julian Rotter, the more we see a connection between what we do and what happens to us, the more *internally controlled* we are. In contrast, the less we see a connection between what we do and what happens to us—i.e., the more we view the things that happen to us as outside of our influence—the more *externally controlled* we are.

Differences in this fundamental way of looking at what happens to us in our world can have an unbelievably powerful impact on how we behave. If we are internally controlled and involved in a relationship, for example, we are more likely to pay attention to what is going on in that relationship because we believe that the information we pick up and send will be useful to us in making that relationship succeed. In contrast, if we are externally controlled, we're not going to be as attentive to what is going on because we have come to believe that our actions will have little or no impact on the ongoing relationship—a sure prescription for relationship failure.

For the past thirty years, we have been studying locus of control. We have developed scales to measure locus of control in children as young as three and in adults as old as a hundred. The scales have been used in over one thousand studies and in thirty-four countries. One of the most common characteristics of being dyssemic is having an external locus of control. Why? Because if you are failing interpersonally due to being dyssemic, you probably are not aware that it is your nonverbal shortcomings that are the source. Instead, it appears to you that no matter what you attempt to do to make relationships work, it doesn't succeed. It is these kinds of experiences that can lead people to feel as though there is no connection between what they do and what happens to them.

Copy the Locus of Control scale and fill it out for yourself, then use the scoring key and scoring instructions located in Appendix A. Calculate your score before you read further.

A Measure of Your Belief in Your Ability to Control What Happens to You

We are trying to find out how much of a connection you see between what you do and what happens to you. We want you to answer the following questions the way you feel. There are no right or wrong answers. Don't take too much time answering any one question, but do try to answer them all, and try to pick one or the other response for all the questions and not leave any blank.

One of your concerns during the test may be, "What should I do if I can answer both yes and no to a question?" It's not unusual for that to happen. If it does, think about whether your answer is just a little more one way than the other. For example, if you'd assign a weight of 51 percent to "yes" and assign 49 percent to "no," then make your answer "yes."

_____ 1. Do you believe that most problems will solve themselves if you just don't fool with them?

_____ 2. Do you believe that you can stop yourself from catching a cold?

_____ 3. Are some people just born lucky?

_____ 4. In school, did you feel most of the time that getting good grades meant a great deal to you?

_____ 5. Are you often blamed for things that aren't your fault?

_____ 6. Do you believe that if somebody studies hard enough he or she can pass any subject?

_____ 7. Do you feel that most of the time it doesn't pay to try hard because things never turn out right anyway?

_____ 8. Do you feel that if things start out well in the morning it's going to be a good day, no matter what you do?

_____ 9. Do you feel that most of the time parents listen to what their children have to say?

_____ 10. Do you believe that wishing can make good things happen?

_____ 11. When you get reprimanded, does it usually seem it's for no good reason at all?

_____ 12. Most of the time, do you find it hard to change a friend's opinion?

_____ 13. Do you think that cheering more than luck helps a team to win?

_____ 14. Did you feel that it was nearly impossible to change your parents' minds about anything?

_____ 15. Do you believe that parents should allow children to make most of their own decisions?

_____ 16. Do you feel that when you do something wrong there's very little you can do to make it right?

_____ 17. Do you believe that most people who are good at sports are just born that way?

_____ 18. Are most of the other people your age stronger than you are?

_____ 19. Do you feel that one of the best ways to handle most problems is just not to think about them?

_____ 20. Do you feel that you have a lot of choice in deciding who your friends are?

_____ 21. If you find a four-leaf clover, do you believe that it might bring you good luck?

_____ 22. Did you often feel that whether or not you did your homework had much to do with what kind of grades you got?

_____ 23. Do you feel that when a person is angry with you, there's little you can do to stop him or her?

_____ 24. Have you ever had a good-luck charm?

_____ 25. Do you believe that whether or not people like you depends on how you act?

_____ 26. Did your parents usually help you if you asked them to?

_____ 27. Have you felt that when people were angry with you it was usually for no good reason at all?

_____ 28. Most of the time, do you feel that you can change what might happen tomorrow by what you do today?

_____ 29. Do you believe that when bad things are going to happen they are just going to happen, no matter what you try to do to stop them?

_____ 30. Do you think that people can get their own way if they just keep trying?

_____ 31. Most of the time, did you find it useless to try and get your own way at home?

_____ 32. Do you feel that when good things happen they happen because of hard work?

_____ 33. Do you feel that when somebody wants to be your enemy there's little you can do to change matters?

_____ 34. Do you feel that it's easy to get friends to do what you want them to do?

_____ 35. Do you usually feel that you have little to say about what you get to eat at home?

_____ 36. Do you feel that when someone doesn't like you there's little you can do about it?

_____ 37. Did you usually feel that it was almost useless to try in school because most other children were just plain smarter than you were?

_____ 38. Are you the kind of person who believes that planning ahead makes things turn out better?

_____ 39. Most of the time, do you feel that you have little to say about what your family decides to do?

_____ 40. Do you think it's better to be smart than to be lucky?

Now score your test using the key provided in Appendix A.

What Does Your Score Mean?

Low Scorers (0 to 8): Scores from zero to eight represent the range for about one third of the people taking the test. As a low scorer, you probably see life as a game of skill rather than chance. You most likely believe that you have a lot of control over what happens to you, both good and bad. You tend to take the initiative in everything from job-related activities to relationships. You are probably described by others as vigilant in getting things done, aware of what's going on around you, and willing to spend energy in working for specific goals. You would probably find it quite frustrating to sit back and let others take care of you, since your test answers stressed that you like to have your life in your own hands.

Although taking control of your life is seen by most people as the best way to be, psychologists caution that it has its own potential set of difficulties. Someone who is responsible for his or her own successes is also responsible for failures. So if you scored high in this direction, be prepared for the downs as well as the ups.

Average Scorers (9 to 16): Since you've answered some of the questions in each direction, your beliefs about internal and external control may be situation specific. You may look at one situation—work, for example—and believe that your rewards are externally determined, that no matter what you do you can't get ahead. In another situation—love, perhaps—you may see your fate as resting entirely in your own hands. You will find it helpful to review the questions and group them into those you answered in the internal direction and those you answered it the external direction. Are there any similarities in the kinds of situations within one of the groups? If so, some time spent thinking about what aspects of those situations make you feel as though the control is or is not in your hands can help you better understand yourself.

High Scorers (17 to 40): Scores in this range represent the external control end of the scale. It has been found that only about 15 percent of the people taking the test score 17 or higher. As a high scorer, you're saying that you see life generally more as a game of chance than as one where your skills make a difference.

There are many different reasons for any individual to score in the external control direction. For example, psychologists have found that people in many minority and disadvantaged groups tend to score in the external direction. One recent suggestion for such scores is that people in these groups perceive their life situations realistically. In general, many minorities and members of lower socioeconomic classes really do have more restrictions on their own successes—fewer job options, lower pay, and less opportunity for advancement in many cases, no matter what they do or don't do. An internal locus of control belief in such situations would be quite unrealistic and inappropriate. Thus, your own high external control score could be a realistic perception of your current life circumstances.

On the other hand, your score may represent a strong belief in luck or superstition and a concurrent feeling of helplessness in controlling your life. Research studies have shown a relation between unrealistic external control beliefs and problems like anxiety, depression, low self-concept, and poor physical health. Only you can decide exactly how much of your external belief system is accurate and how much of it is inappropriate given your life situation.

What Does Locus of Control Have to Do with Relationships?

Research on the locus of control scale that you have just taken has shown that internals tend to be better adjusted, have more friends and enjoy longer-lasting friendships, and experience more successful marriages, among other things. Internals probably do better at relationships because they believe in their efforts to make them better. In contrast, externals have more trouble dealing with others because they don't see a connection between their behavior and the way their relationships will go. Over time, if you are dyssemic, chances are you will become more external because you believe your actions—that is, your attempts to be friendly and engage others—don't seem to make any difference in how things turn out. This, of course, is far from true; in fact, your being dyssemic and your lack of awareness of that fact is the very reason you may be having relationship problems. One of the keys to changing external control expectancies, as it is to correcting dyssemia and reducing anxiety, is being aware of what is going on in your interpersonal life so you can learn how to interact better over time.

The Self: How We Become Who We Are

Our "self" concept comes primarily from what psychologist Harry Stack Sullivan called the "reflected appraisals of significant others." More simply put, our self develops from how we notice others reacting to us. Sometime during the first year of our life, we become aware that there are others around us, usually adults, who are reacting to us. Depending on how others are responding to us, we begin to get an inkling of who we are, and our self-concept starts to form. If we think others are reacting in positive ways to us—i.e., they are smiling, nodding approval, and showing us in other ways that we are a "good" person—then we are soon going to conclude that we must be a good person, and a positive self-concept begins to form. However, we are likely to draw the opposite conclusion about our self if we notice others responding negatively to us in the form of frowns, angry looks, or disapproving noises. These are the raw materials that go into the development of a self-concept as a "bad" one.

The initial and most important significant other from whom we receive feedback about what we're like is our mother, but our feedback group can quickly grow to include others who are important to us as we grow and develop. Since we do not begin to develop effective verbal language until we are about eighteen months to two years of age, our initial reflected appraisals are communicated and received nonverbally. This is shown nicely in the following experience.

What's Andy's Self-Concept Likely to Be?

Six-month-old Andy had just finished with his bath and was lying on the dressing table while his father powdered him. As he sprinkled powder on the baby, the father was making exaggerated faces and sounds. Andy was responding to these behaviors by making sounds back, smiling and thrashing about with his arms and legs. "Whoosee little boo boo is you? Whoosee, whoosee, whoosee, whoosee!" he cooed, to the seeming delight of Andy, whose own responses ignited another round of exaggerated facial expressions and nonsensical sounds and smiles from the both of them.

Based on what is going on nonverbally, chances are good that Andy is well on his way to a very positive self-concept. What's interesting is that nonverbal communication continues to significantly determine if we feel good or bad about our selves even after we learn how to use verbal language and speech.

Shaping Our Sense of Self: Relationships throughout Childhood

Our self-concept, though always open to change, is most flexible and likely to change when we are younger. What we think about our self is in turn, reflected by how successful we are at making our relationships work out as we grow up. We must learn how to form positive relationships first with our family members, next with our childhood peers, and finally with our adult peers.

Verbal Language

Developmentally, verbal language arrives like a supernova, blurring out everything else that the child is doing. Children's first words are recorded in books and relatives are called to share the good news. With verbal language, we can compare our ideas with those of others to see if we agree with how they think or feel about interpersonal events that have taken place. This *consensual validation* allows us to correct mistakes about interpersonal events and to learn to behave, feel, and think in ways that are similar to others.

Peer Relationships

What we learned in our own family homes about interactions is tested mightily when we take our quest for relationships out into the school situation. School is a great place for us to learn more about how to be interpersonally effective and, through the process of consensual validation, to correct any inappropriate verbal and nonverbal communications that we might have learned in our home.

The "Chum" Relationship

If all goes as it should, sometime between around nine and twelve years of age we develop a close relationship with a peer that is intimate but not sexual. Many of us may remember a "chum" from our own childhood, a friend with whom we developed a uniquely close relationship. We probably spent what others considered too much time talking, visiting, giggling, and doing things with our chum. Our chum was important because he or she helped us to understand what was happening in our shared interpersonal world.

What Are Chums Like? Steve and Ken

Steve and Ken were eleven years old and attended Center Street Elementary School. They walked to and from school together, played on the school softball team, and sat side by side in class. Their teacher, Mr. Mellon, often joked that they seemed to be joined at the hip because they could always be found together. Often, after they returned to their respective homes, one would call the other and they would rehash the day's events. It was during these phone calls that they would decide all matter of things, like whether they should be angry or not with certain classmates, or whether the new girl was cute and if she liked either one of them. Sometimes their discussions would focus on which way to wear their baseball caps to look the "coolest." Other times they would tell one another to stop acting goofy about something that happened and accept that they were wrong. But when all was said and done, they were utterly devoted to one another and each would often put the happiness of the other ahead of their own.

The commitment to sacrifice our own needs for those of our chum, as Steve and Ken were learning to do, has its compensation. The chum relationship offers a unique opportunity for consensual validation and for correcting errors in interpersonal behavior that can prepare us for making more and better friends in the future.

We would suspect that many of you who are dyssemic may not have experienced a very successful chum stage. If you had, your chum would have offered you the kind of helpful feedback that would have corrected your nonverbal botches and mistakes. Failing to develop a chum relationship has a serious downside: You can feel both alone and lonely. True loneliness only becomes possible at the chum stage. This is the age when we are smart enough to understand what we are losing when we fail to have a truly close friend. Our guess is that if you are dyssemic you may have vivid and unpleasant memories of how it felt to be lonely and not fit in.

Sexualized Relationships

Adolescence begins with the onset of puberty, and sexuality suddenly becomes a very potent force in how we develop our relationships. One day the opposite sex is "yucky" and the next it is a mystery that has great power. Before we know what's happening, we feel ourselves being pushed to seek intimacy with selected other individuals. Very few of us know exactly how to do that at the beginning. Having a chum with whom we can discuss our ongoing attempts at relating to the intimate others makes it all so much easier.

At the end of adolescence we begin our transition into adulthood. If all has gone well we will have learned the interpersonal skills necessary for developing stable, intimate relationships with others, both nonsexual and sexual. But the story does not end there, because it turns out that adulthood is filled with opportunities for continued interpersonal growth if we learn to communicate well by both verbal and nonverbal means. However, if we have not developed adequate skills in nonverbal communication—the language of the heart and the relationship—the same problems that we experienced in childhood and adolescence can continue to plague us. The big difference is that the problems can now extend beyond the social domain and enter our work lives.

We've covered a lot in this chapter. You should have a sense of your interpersonal skillfulness, your locus of control, and your level of anxiety. However, before we move forward to step two and our attack on your dyssemia itself, there is still some basic information you need. It's waiting for you in the next chapter.

Chapter 2

The Four Stages of Interpersonal Relationships

To continue to help you to figure out if you are dyssemic or not, we need to take a closer look at the "lifetime" of your relationships and what part problems in nonverbal communication play in them. We want to describe the way we believe relationships operate so that you can be more accurate in determining the range and site of your dyssemias and how they may be affecting your attempts to relate to others.

We believe that relationships go through a predictable process of stability and change in phases that we call by the nontechnical terms *choice, beginning, deepening,* and *ending.* To successfully make a transition from one phase of a relationship to the next, participants must communicate with one another. Though most of us would agree that communication is important in making relationships work, in the past we tended to focus more on verbal communication, as though words in and of themselves were the avenue to interpersonal success. (We think that we were all looking under the lamppost 'cause the light was better there!) Our view is quite different. We believe that expertise in another language, the nonverbal one, is necessary for our relationship success. Don't get us wrong, verbal language is critically important! However, we have come to believe that verbal language is more the language of the mind and the classroom. Nonverbal language, we propose, is the language of how we feel about ourselves and others.

Like automobiles or the human circulatory system, relationships must be understood as complex things that have identifiable parts and functions. Once you know their parts and how they are supposed to fit and work together, you will be able to identify successful versus unsuccessful ones and know how to fix the ones that aren't working so well. We'll begin our examination of the anatomy of relationships with the choice phase.

Stage One: The Choice Phase

We will meet some 50,000 people in our lives, and from among these we must choose several with whom to pursue a relationship. Nowhere is the process of choosing with whom to begin a relationship more obvious than at the beginning of the school year at any college. Thousands of young adults all over the country arrive at colleges where they know few other people. If they don't want to remain a loner for very long, they must begin to connect with others. But with whom should they choose to initiate a relationship? The stakes are high. They may be choosing someone who will turn out to be their best friend or worst enemy. We believe their choices will be governed primarily by their ability to use nonverbal language.

While the beginning of a school year on a college campus is one place to see choice in action, it is, of course, going on day in and day out everywhere—in offices, meetings, and parties. We know making a choice can be done very quickly. In fact, it only takes about seven seconds to form a positive or negative judgment about another person. Obviously, since few words are spoken, this judgement is based primarily on what we observe nonverbally. Once we make our choice, we can get on with beginning.

Stage Two: The Beginning Phase

We need both verbal and nonverbal skill to begin a relationship successfully. Fortunately, this is a stage of relating where we get some help. In fact, our culture provides a learnable and widely taught set of rules called "etiquette" or "manners" that define acceptable behavior for beginning relationships with others.

Beginning a Relationship—Nakita

Nakita was feeling very lost on her first day of orientation at college. Before she knew it, a woman about her height and dressed in tan slacks and blue T-shirt walked up to her, smiled, held out her hand, and said, "Hello, my name is Cloris. Are you taking part in orientation?" Nakita smiled back, took Cloris's offered hand in her own, shook it, and said, "Yes, it's all so overwhelming though, isn't it?" "Yes," said Cloris, "but you'll get used to it. I'm from Chicago. Where are you from?" Soon Nakita and Cloris were in a lively conversation with each other about where they were from, what the weather was like, and what courses they were going to be taking.

What had just transpired was a traditional and accepted form that many of us use to begin a new relationship. We smile, we offer our hand for a handshake, and we usually say some polite form of "Pleased to meet you." This is typically followed by small talk tailored to fit the occasion. In this instance, Cloris and Nakita could choose from a variety of small talk topics, including what parts of the country they were from, what they were hoping to major in, and what the rest of the day might bring. Most of us are taught to begin relationships in this same manner. Consider for a moment how you would react to anyone you met who didn't use any of the above behaviors required for beginning a relationship. This was Roderick's problem.

Problems in Beginning a Relationship—Roderick

Roderick was a big, lumbering, 220-pound man who was thirty-five years of age. He liked to wear his hair long and natural so that it hung wildly around his face. When he walked, his hair jumped up and down and all around. Roderick thought he looked "neat." Roderick was a kind and nice man. He often volunteered at a downtown mission's soup kitchen and he gave at least 10 percent of what he made from his construction work to charities. What Roderick didn't know how to do was begin a relationship in a new setting. For some reason he had never learned what most of the rest of his colleagues and acquaintances knew about beginning relationships with others. When in a new situation and meeting new people, he would just stand there and stare as people introduced themselves to him. His behavior flustered others and when they tried to recover by beginning some small talk about the weather or current events, Roderick just answered "yes" or "no" or grunted something unintelligible. Because of his size and appearance, people rarely got angry with Roderick's seemingly boorish behavior or had the nerve to tell him how he was affecting them. As a result, Roderick never got the feedback he needed to know how negatively he was affecting others, and as a consequence he had few friends. Only those individuals who were forced to stay in relationships with him got to know that he really was a good guy.

Based on our clinical experience, those of you who have problems in the beginning of relationships generally have one of the following two kinds of difficulties, or both. First, you may have made some poor decisions in choosing with whom to begin a relationship. Second, even if you made a good choice, you may lack the skills to start a conversation and present topics appropriate to keep the relationship going during its very early stages. As mentioned earlier, the choice of conversational content is usually something that is taught to us over and over again and, depending on the particular situation, can include one's job, hometown, schools attended, leisure-time activities, weather, and common interests. Our attempts to begin a relationship will be short-lived if we begin them with questions about clothing size or casual sex. Regardless of the reasons, if you have problems in beginning relationships, you are likely to have many more short- than long-term encounters.

Stage Three: The Deepening Phase

Have you ever noticed how most people who have advice for you about how to meet new people become strangely quiet when you ask them how to make these new acquaintances into close intimate partners? If you have successfully managed to choose and begin with someone, you must now deal with a much more difficult task: deepening. Of the thousands of people you meet during your lifetime, only a select handful will manage to become close friends or intimate sexual partners. How these few individuals make it past all of your barriers to become so close is largely a mystery to us. You won't get much help from other people in solving this mystery either. Amy, the three-times-engaged woman we met in the introduction, could not make the transition to a truly deep and long-lasting relationship with a man. Kyle ended up going to Cubs' games by himself and sitting with strangers because he had no close friends. Unlike in the beginning phase, where what we need to say and do is taught directly to us by our culture, the skills needed to deepen a relationship are less clear.

For you to successfully make the transition from beginning a relationship to deepening it, two things are essential. First, you must spend sufficient time in the beginning phase before you decide to deepen it. What you may not be aware of is that your decision is based primarily on information carried by nonverbal cues that have been exchanged. Nonverbal communication of closeness usually precedes any verbal declarations of a deepening relationship. You may smile more or stand closer to the other person, who in turn returns your smile and doesn't move away. In some cultures, individuals signal the change from an acquaintance to a friend relationship by changing the verbal forms of the language—in German, for example, by using the "du" form of address instead of the "Sie" form, both indicating "you," but with different degrees of familiarity. In any case and in any verbal or nonverbal language, we have found that dyssemia makes the already difficult task of deepening a relationship a nearly impossible one.

Because of the complexities involved in deepening, we marvel that we aren't all more like Kyle and Amy, continually knocking on the door of deeper relationships with others but never being asked to come in. For those of you who have not yet had your knocking answered, we urge you not to lose heart but to continue to persist, because the benefits of being in a deep relationship are numerous. People who are in deep relationships live longer, recover more quickly from illnesses, and are generally happier and more secure. All of these benefits and more can be yours if you can get beyond relationship beginnings and deepen your connections with at least one other significant person in your life.

Stage Four: The Ending Phase

Nearly all us have difficulties ending relationships appropriately. Because endings are so difficult, most of us avoid them by getting busy or by getting angry with those we are about to part from, to reduce the pain of separation. One of this book's authors, Steve, teaches a seminar on relationships to second-semester seniors at Emory. In this seminar, one important goal is to help the students learn how to end their relationships in general through the way they handle the end of their four years at Emory and the change in relationships with the significant people they've known there. Seniors know when they are freshmen that their relationship with Emory will end at graduation four years later. Yet it is like pulling teeth without painkillers to get these bright, articulate men and women students to even talk about ending, let alone to acknowledge that their relationship with Emory is quickly drawing to a close. Steve's teaching goal is to help his students prepare for their ending by dealing with all the people in their lives at Emory they would like to recognize, thank, and make sure they say good-bye to. The reward for all this work is that as the students end well with others, they learn what they did right and what they did wrong in their past relationships so they can use that knowledge to develop better relationships for themselves in the future.

Sometimes events outside of a relationship will signal its end. For example, the birth of a first child signals that the relationship that existed between husband and wife before the child's arrival has ended. The couple must now get on with the task of *choosing to begin* a new relationship with one another while living with and "serving" a third person. However, after ending, and with your return to the choice and beginning phases of a relationship, you are also returning to the anxieties, insecurities, and doubts that characterize these transitions. It is important for you to understand that anxious and uncomfortable feelings are normal at these times and do not indicate that the prior relationship was bad or that the new relationship will fail. Coauthor Marshall's wife decided at age forty to train for a career as a learning disability specialist, and Steve's wife opted at age fifty to begin a new career by entering theology school and training to become a chaplain. Such life-changing decisions are to be expected during adulthood. In both cases, we discussed the implications of these decisions for our relationships because we knew that they signaled the end of our relationships as they existed and marked transitions to the beginning of new ones. The point is that all long-term relationships will go through a number of choice, beginning, deepening, and ending cycles.

Ending can be the most important phase in the relationship process, the only time when you can look back over the full course of your interactions with another person and learn which elements of what you experienced with him or her can be applied to your next relationship, either with that same person or with someone else. Awareness of what you have experienced in relationships is necessary if you are ever going to improve your ability to relate to others and to grow as a psychological being. Lack of awareness dooms you to repeat relationship mistakes. In fact, even knowing when and how to end a bad relationship can be a positive thing, especially if what is learned will lessen the chances that another bad relationship will follow.

If ending a relationship is so important, what skills are necessary for the process to be successful? As in the deepening phase, success depends on congruent verbal and nonverbal communication and sensitivity to nonverbal signs that the relationship may be coming to an end. People who have trouble ending typically talk about feeling "trapped" or "going in circles." The skills that help us through endings involve being *aware* that the relationship is ending. The awareness usually arrives in the form of a sensed change in the "feel" of the interaction. Some people have compared ending a relationship to taking a friend to the airport after an extended visit. In anticipation of the boarding announcement, you hug one another and say good-bye. Imagine how you'd then feel if, after all this, the plane is delayed, leaving you uncomfortably standing with the person to whom you've already said good-bye. This feeling is what we are talking about: The relationship is over and people should have left, but there they still are.

The idea of ending well and moving on to new relationships is shown nicely by one of our all-time favorite movie actors, Humphrey Bogart. Remember the end of the wonderful movie *Casablanca?* Bogart has finally ended his relationship with Ingrid Bergman, who has just flown off with her husband into the night sky. As the plane becomes a speck of light and then disappears, Bogart marks the ending of one relationship and the moving on to others by turning to Claude Rains, who is playing the French policeman who's just offered to arrange passage for both of them to the site of a Free French garrison, and saying, "Louis, I think this is the beginning of a beautiful friendship." We could not agree more with his attitude of ending well and moving on to new choices and new beginnings.

The Johari Window

To continue in our quest to help you determine if you are dyssemic we introduce an exotic-sounding but important practical concept called the *Johari Window,* named after its originators, Joseph Luft and Harry Ingham (Jo-Har-I), two midwestern psychologists. The "window" is actually four squares that reflect differences in what information is known *to us* about us and what information is known *to others* about us.

Box one, located in the upper left-hand corner of the four squares, is labeled "open." In this box is information that is known both to you and to others. Examples would be the color of the shirt or blouse you are wearing while talking with someone, or the objects (like shopping bags) you are carrying as you walk through a crowded shopping mall.

In contrast to the open access and awareness of the flow of information between you and others in box one, box two contains "hidden" information that is only available to you and not to others. An example would be your awareness that you do not like

The Johari Window

Box One Known to Self Known to Others (Open)	**Box Two** Known to Self Unknown to Others (Hidden)
Box Three Unknown to Self Known to Others (Blind)	**Box Four** Unknown to Self Unknown to Others (Unknown)

another person whom you have met in a social setting. Chances are the person you dislike does not realize your feelings because social etiquette dictates that you act in a courteous way to everyone. Another box-two example would be your knowledge of events that happened in your past of which others are not aware. A true box-two situation includes only thoughts and feelings that *in fact* are not known to others and are known only by you. When there are thoughts, events, and/or feelings that we *think* are not known to others, but which actually are, we are no longer in box two but probably in a different box, box three.

In box three of the Johari Window we find information that others know about us but that is unknown to us. From reading the introduction and chapter 1, you can see that much of what we've written about nonverbal behavior up to now might fall here. A physical example is like having a clothing tag showing on the back of your shirt or blouse. A box-three interpersonal event might be erroneously communicating sadness through your facial expression when you believe you're appearing happy. Interactions flavored by the characteristics of box three can be confusing and anxiety-producing, and are prime candidates for failure. So long as information remains known to others but not to you, the potential for you experiencing interpersonal trouble remains high. If both participants become aware of the fact that erroneous information is being exchanged, the interaction can then be reclassified as belonging in box one and can more easily be dealt with.

The fourth and last quadrant in the Johari Window, box four, is the one labeled "unknown." Here is information about you that is unknown both to you and to others. This might remind you somewhat of Freud's concept of the unconscious mind, but it actually includes a great deal of other material that can easily be brought into conscious awareness, such as—you guessed it—nonverbal communication.

The Johari Window and Examples of Dyssemia

As we pointed out in the introduction, dyssemias have their impact on relationships because they are continuous, have a negative emotional impact, and, most importantly, take place out of awareness. Using the Johari Window allows us to look more specifically at how differences in level of awareness can affect interpersonal encounters. If there is awareness on both sides of an interaction, damage is minimized and opportunities for reconciliation are increased (box one). Likewise, if we are aware of what we are doing interpersonally and satisfactorily mask our negative feelings when they occur (in keeping with social etiquette), our chances of significant interpersonal difficulty are lessened (box two). However, box three and box four present more disquieting communication possibilities. When people lack awareness of their inaccuracy either in sending or receiving (box three), then the likelihood of interpersonal difficulties caused by these inaccuracies increases. One example would be Amy, who did not know that she was wearing an angry facial expression, while her customers clearly did. Finally, the highest risk interpersonally exists when there are dyssemias and both participants lack awareness of what is going on nonverbally (box four). Here we find an example in the negative effect that Kyle had on Ruth and Rosita. All of them felt that their interactions were unsatisfying, but none of them knew why.

The Johari Window helps us to identify common forms of dyssemia that can be corrected through our three-step program. The absence of awareness on the part of the person with dyssemia that is common to both box three and box four creates most of the interpersonal problems that he or she faces.

Box Three Problems

Box three dyssemics are people who believe that they are doing just fine with other people but who are unaware that they have a nonverbal problem that is holding them back. The Scottish poet Robert Burns wrote a poem called "Ode to a Louse." He wrote, "O wad some Power the giftie gie us / To see oursels as ithers see us!" In modern parlance, Burns's wish was for someone to give us the ability to see ourselves as others do and to benefit from that special knowledge usually denied to us. For us, Burns's wish represents the need for input from others about how we come across to them. In the past, being told how you were doing by parents, teachers, and friends seemed to be a more common experience than it is today. The reasons for this may be that social rules are more fluid and society more fluid, but it is unfortunate that we don't get more feedback from others about things we do that annoy or bother them. We've taken to calling instances where we've received this kind of unexpected but helpful feedback "Robert Burns Moments." One such moment is described next.

One of the Authors and His Secretary

When Marshall was director of the graduate program in clinical psychology at Emory University, he had the privilege of working with a very special woman named Rosemary, who served as his administrative assistant. Rosemary was an ideal coworker who knew what needed to be done and did it with style and competence. Students sought her out as a confidante and spent many an hour pouring out to her their frustrations and disappointments regarding their studies. She was liked and trusted by all. One afternoon, Marshall was chatting with Rosemary about a talk he had just given and she told him that she thought he had done a wonderful job. Being unable to take compliments easily, Marshall quipped how lucky he was that his audience's only choice was between listening to his talk or watching a hardware truck unload at the local Sears Roebuck (implying that they liked his talk because everything else was *really* boring). At that comment, Rosemary, in uncharacteristically direct fashion, said, "Close the door for a minute." Sensing that he was about to hear something for his ears alone, Marshall complied. As soon as they were alone in the office, Rosemary said, "Listen, buster, when someone gives you a compliment, don't go on with all this crap about how they are too dumb to know otherwise or that you are such a lucky guy that they had you rather than something really boring. That cheapens their feelings. Just say 'Thank you' and shut up! Now open the door."

Marshall was dumfounded. Rosemary had taken a chance at telling him about something he did that put people off. This was a true Robert Burns Moment. He has not forgotten Rosemary's message, and has never again tried to talk people out of their feelings or resisted compliments. He simply replies "Thank you" appropriately.

Box Four Problems

Sometimes dyssemias cause people problems and neither they nor anyone around them know where they come from. Being unknown to everyone involved, such problems become box-four situations. People find themselves in situations where they are failing interpersonally, but don't have a clue as to why. One common way that this can happen is when previously successful nonverbal language patterns are used in new situations to which they are ill-suited.

In contrast to the box-three example, where the person involved is not really aware of a problem, in box-four dyssemia, people are experiencing noticeable discomfort, continuous frustration, and/or unexplainable failures in their social or vocational efforts, but they and those around them are unaware that the problems are caused by their own nonverbal behavior. In our first example of such box-four dyssemia, the reason for the problem is the misapplication of previously successful nonverbal behaviors to a new situation where those patterns are no longer adaptive. We think that you will get a good flavor of what we mean with the following example of Warren, a fifty-two-year-old elementary school principal from Eugene, Oregon.

Warren

Warren had been an assistant principal in his school for ten years and was promoted to principal when his old friend and longtime colleague, Barry, retired. Warren was well qualified for the job. He knew every nook and cranny in the school building and had excellent relationships with all of the teachers, the office staff, and the maintenance staff. Everyone was overjoyed at his appointment. Two months into the school year, however, Warren found himself spending more and more time in his office alone with the door closed. He felt estranged even from some of the people he had previously felt closest to. He had no idea about what was going on. He did the only thing he could think of: He called Barry and asked him out to lunch.

A principal for the better part of a quarter century, Barry had a pretty good sense of what was wrong. He had experienced it himself and had seen it happen to many other people who had moved up the ranks of the school system. Barry's term for it was "growing pains," but we saw it as something quite different, called *situational dyssemia*. The situation was this: Warren had come to his new job with a set of interpersonal skills and patterns that were extremely effective for an assistant principal. The problem was, he wasn't an assistant principal anymore. Barry told him that he had to learn a whole new set of rules. We'll mention just a few. He had to learn new rules of space usage—when he came into a room, the teachers were no longer calmed because it was Warren, the nice assistant principal; they were now tense because it was Warren, the principal who was doing their evaluations. He had to learn new rules of touch—even the most innocent of touches could be interpreted as inappropriate or threatening, even if he did not mean it that way. His voice tone needed to be more leader-like and less assistant-like. Essentially, Barry told him, the patterns of his relationship style, while not needing to change totally or even dramatically, needed to be seriously examined.

Warren realized that Barry was right and began observing not only his own behavior but also that of the teachers and staff. Even his old friends tended to give him more space than they used to. People talked to him in a more formal way. They did not walk into his office freely, as they had when he was the assistant principal. It took one year for Warren to begin to master the new nonverbal language patterns of a school principal. The same phenomenon can be observed in other situational dyssemia situations, such as promotion in a business or change in the stages of relationships between people. What works in one situation does not always work in others. To be fully functioning in nonverbal language is (just as in verbal language) to know that a situation has changed, to be able to identify the new patterns needed in the new situation, and to be able to develop these patterns over time.

Simply having a significant dyssemia will gain you entrance to box four. With Warren, the dyssemia was situational. The most common form of box-four dyssemia is caused by some inherent personal shortcoming or absence of social skill. You have already seen an example of someone with this kind of box-four dyssemia in our description of Kyle, the well-meaning engineer you met at the start of this book, who had so much trouble relating to people in his office. Allow us to tell you a bit more about him now, because we are going to travel some way with him throughout the rest of this book.

Kyle

Kyle was a thirty-seven-year-old chemical engineer working with a large corporation developing processes for extracting certain compounds from natural products. Isolated through much of his life, Kyle was feeling that with his advancing age, his chances of finding someone to share his life with were growing progressively slimmer, while he himself was growing progressively heavier, balder, and more set in his ways. Dates were usually frustrating experiences and rarely did he have the opportunity to see a woman a second time. Kyle actually wrote us an e-mail after he saw an article about our work in his local newspaper. He told us a story of a life filled with frustration, false starts, and rejections. We called him and spoke with him on the phone.

With his permission, we recorded our phone conversations. We often do this if there might be a problem in paralanguage, very common in people who have trouble getting past beginning with others. We noticed that Kyle spoke as if he were a recording in an airport, making the same dull, emotionless announcement about "no food in the transportation mall" over and over. It was the kind of paralanguage message that conveyed that he was bored and that if you continued interacting with him, you soon would be also.

Few people are aware of how they sound to others, and we suspected that no one had ever told Kyle about his impact. Now however, he had put himself in a position where we could help him. He used our program of self-help—the very same program that we will be describing for you in chapters 6, 7, and 8.

Kyle's dyssemias were the sources of his unsatisfactory interpersonal interactions and relationships. Because his problems were located in box four, he could benefit most from being made aware of his deficiencies and the way relationships are supposed to work. Kyle was a well-intentioned person. He had professional skills that made him a desirable employee. He had many positive social attributes. He liked to be with people. He wanted someday to be a good husband and father. His problem was that he had not learned well the second language that we all must speak—the language of nonverbal signs.

With the knowledge you have gained in the introduction and the first two chapters, it should be easier for you to determine if you are dyssemic and where problems in nonverbal communication are generally affecting your relationships. We get even more specific about the type of dyssemia you may be experiencing in the next three chapters, where we describe the full rich range of human nonverbal behavior and complete what you need to know to adequately assess if you are dyssemic in one or more channels.

Chapter 3

Channels of Nonverbal Behavior: Rhythm, Time, and Space

The basic channels of rhythm, use of time (chronemics), and use of space (proxemics) are fascinating because, even more than other types of nonverbal behavior, they tend to operate largely removed from our awareness and in the background of relationships. But don't let their relative anonymity fool you. As you will see, these diffuse nonverbal behaviors are among the most important inhabitants of the Johari box four, exerting enormous influence on what takes place between us.

Rhythm

The Importance of Rhythm—Antonio

It had not been a very good day for Antonio, and he didn't expect the night's cocktail party to be any better. Antonio was a second-year math teacher at a middle school in Charlotte, North Carolina. He and his wife had moved to Charlotte from the Midwest because they had heard it was an up-and-coming city with plenty of good jobs. Even as a small child, Antonio had always wanted to be a teacher, and most of the time he considered himself extremely fortunate to be doing what he always wanted to do—but that had not been how he felt earlier in the day as he tried to teach. Even when they are at their best, middle-school children have trouble focusing on academics for very long, and that day they had not been at their best. In class after class, his students fidgeted and squirmed until Antonio felt like screaming for them all to sit still. But he was too good a teacher to do that. He gave each class his best effort, but the day just dragged on and on.

And what reward did he receive for his daylong efforts to teach? Did he get to play tennis? Did he get to sit in his favorite easy chair at home and read that new Michael Crichton novel? No, he got to do none of those things. Instead, what he got to do was go to this boring cocktail party being hosted by his wife's new boss at the insurance company where she worked. The last thing he wanted to do was to make small talk with strangers, and he was carefully biding his time until he could make a quick and quiet exit to get home to his chair. He found himself at the punch bowl getting what he hoped would be his final drink before leaving when he literally bumped into another man who was also getting a drink. "Sorry," Antonio said. "No problem, you betcha," the other man said.

For some reason, rather than turning and walking away to continue his plans for an early escape, Antonio found himself continuing to talk to the stranger. "Yeah, it's hard to concentrate on getting a drink and still make sure one of these guys doesn't sneak up behind you, tap you on the shoulder, and try to talk you into buying some life insurance." The minute he said this Antonio felt embarrassed because maybe this guy sold life insurance, but before he could apologize, the other man said, "I know just what you mean. I'm Jerry Blanfield. My wife and I just moved here from Minnesota and it's been kinda tough getting to know people."

Antonio said with a delighted smile, "Where in Minnesota? I'm from outside Minneapolis myself, a little town called Northfield."

"Now, I'm from just north of Minneapolis," answered Jerry.

The conversation continued in both an animated and relaxed fashion. Soon Antonio and Jerry met one another's wives and Antonio's thoughts about his long, hard day and leaving the party early were forgotten as he enjoyed the company of his new acquaintances.

What magical thing had happened? What had transformed Antonio from behaving like a monk longing to return to his silent monastery into a man suddenly eager and happy to engage in conversation with a stranger? What changed Antonio was rhythm. Rhythm is not what we usually think about when we think about nonverbal communication, but it is, nevertheless, an essential way we connect with other people.

Personal rhythms vary from individual to individual and from one area of our country to another. We see this in the students we teach at Emory. Many are from the Northeast and about the same number call the South home. Talk about two different rhythms! At first, the fast-moving and faster-talking Yankees and the slow-moving and slower-talking southerners mix like oil and water. Each group initially makes inaccurate personality attributions about the other group based primarily on their differences in rhythm. Southerners see their peers from the northeast not just as faster but as pushy and rude. In return, students from the Northeast view their southern peers not just as slower but as unmotivated and less intelligent. Luckily, once they get to know one another better these attitudes soften and become more reality-based, and friendships form across regional lines.

Most of the time, like the Emory students described above, people are oblivious to their own rhythms or the rhythms of others and how they may be influencing their interactions. The truth is that rhythm can be a powerful force to bring people together or to drive them apart. Similar rhythms brought Antonio and Jerry together. Although he was not aware of it on a conscious level, when Antonio met Jerry he picked up cues of a familiar and compatible rhythm that characterized the area of the country he was from. Before Antonio was aware of it, he was responding favorably to Jerry because of a shared sense of rhythm, and a positive interaction was underway.

We imagine that you, as well, have experienced interactions like Antonio's. You meet someone for the first time and it feels as though you have known him or her for a lifetime. Conversation flows easily and, sure enough, you often find out that your new acquaintance is from the same part of the country. Meeting someone who has the same basic rhythm as you may not guarantee that the relationship will deepen automatically, but it does increase the chances of it getting off to a good start. Likewise, you've probably encountered the opposite scenario as well: meeting someone you dislike instantly even though only a few words have been spoken. Often, discordant rhythm is the culprit here, pushing you away from rather than toward that person.

Rhythm is important because it acts in concert with so many of the other nonverbal channels (like paralanguage, postures, and gestures) and sets the stage for beginning or avoiding the early social interactions with others. In fact, rhythm may very well be the first nonverbal behavior you learn. A classic experiment described by developmental kinesiologist* Walburga von Raffler-Engel makes this point quite eloquently. Von Raffler-Engel was studying the ability of newborn babies to identify and respond to rhythms around them. To evaluate the presence of this skill, she placed a metronome next to the crib of each newborn, setting it to go back and forth at different rates of speed. After testing a number of infants, von Raffler-Engel found that one rate of metronome speed produced sleep in infants faster than any other she tried. Von Raffler-Engel found that only when the metronomes reflected the heart rate of the mother and, therefore, the rhythmic bond already

*Someone who studies movement.

formed between mothers and their infants did the nursery quiet down and the infants fall asleep quickly.

Not only is rhythm important during infancy, it continues to be significantly involved in social behavior ever after. Each of us has our own personal rhythm that accompanies us wherever we go. Some people talk and move faster than others; others always do things more slowly. Maybe your own rhythm is similar to that of your family members, or perhaps you're the odd one out who moves differently than your brothers, sisters, and parents.

Many of you may have left your family of origin for extended times and found out that your new experiences have changed your personal rhythm. How does it feel when you return to visit your family after you've been away? It can oftentimes be a shock to clearly feel what the family rhythm is and how different your rhythm may have become from it. Or perhaps you have tried to go on a trip or vacation with another family or couple and found that your rhythm is completely different from theirs. This can produce the most horrible vacation experience you've ever had or the best, depending on how you deal with the differences.

We cannot overestimate how dyssemia can play havoc with your awareness of your own and others' rhythms. It is easy to become frustrated and even disgusted with someone who is lagging behind and slowing us down. Likewise, people who move quicker than we do and put pressure on us to increase our pace can irritate and anger us. Awareness that it is rhythm differences that is producing the behaviors, and not personal animosity or willfulness, can go a long way to defusing the tension that might develop in these situations.

The ability to read and understand others' nonverbal rhythms is called *receptive rhythm skill,* and the ability to recognize and communicate with our own rhythm and its characteristic speed and tempo is called *expressive rhythm skill.* Both skills are required to be effective interpersonally, and it is possible to be perfectly fine in one but dyssemic in the other.

To be receptively dyssemic for rhythm means that you are unable to accurately read the rhythm of other people or situations. If you are being interviewed for a job, meeting a date for the first time, or having dinner with the boss, it is to your advantage to accurately read the other person's rhythm, because with this information you can make adjustments in your own rhythm. Interpersonally effective people have a range of rhythms by which they can operate, as well as the ability to adjust their rhythm to be in tune with the people they meet.

The second part of the equation, expressing your own rhythm accurately, is as important as the first. The expressive rhythm dyssemic produces a rhythm that is either inappropriate to the situation or dissimilar to that being expressed by others. Because of the nature of nonverbal communication, expressive rhythm dyssemics often are unaware of their own rhythm and how it may be interfering with their attempts to interact with others. As a result, they are surprised and dismayed when they see their attempts to make friends fail. Thinking you are in synch with others when you are not is good recipe for interpersonal failure. See sidebar for an exercise we have devised to help you determine if you have a problem with rhythm.

Are You In or Out of Synch with Others?

- Practice estimating the passage of time. Do this both while you are sitting doing relatively nothing and when you are actively involved in something. See if your estimation is too slow or too fast. This will give you a feel for the kind of errors you might make when you are with others.
- Stop and listen to the rhythms that are going on around you to become sensitive to their existence. For example, while writing this exercise, Steve is aware of many rhythms around him. He can notice:

The humming of the refrigerator and the word processor
Birds calling outside the window, both songbirds and crows that are vocalizing in their own specific rhythms
The meowing of his son and daughter-in-law's cat, whom he is taking care of while they are on a trip
The sound of his fingers tapping on the keys as he types
The wind in the trees signaling the arrival of a much-needed rain in presently drought-parched Georgia
A rhythmic pounding coming from someone making repairs or building an addition to a house in his neighbourhood
The sounds of car tires on the pavement outside

Stopping and paying attention to these rhythms is a good exercise for increasing your own awareness of the existence and potential impact of the many rhythms in and surrounding you.

- When you are walking with people at a mall or going to an event, see if you usually pass more people than pass you, or vice versa. This will be an indication of how the rate of your rhythm stacks up to those of others.
- While waiting in line, ask yourself if you are comfortable with the way the line is moving or if you wish it were moving more quickly.
- Audiotape yourself talking and count how many words you use in a minute. Compare that to the number of words said by others.
- When you are eating, drinking, or engaging in any other activity in the presence of others, note whether you usually finish before, after, or right about the same time as they do.

Regardless of whether you find yourself faster or slower than others, we suggest you practice changing your own rhythm to match that of others. Observe how matching others' rhythms affect them and you.

The Use of Time (Chronemics)

How Time Changes Its Speed—Tanya

Tanya was spending a very nice afternoon with Jim. The sun was finally shining after nearly three days of rain. They had to step around puddles as they walked through the park, but Tanya didn't mind. Quite the contrary, she was having a great time. She had never met anyone like Jim before. He wasn't handsome, but he was cute and so easy to talk to that she barely noticed what he looked like. All she knew was that it was comfortable and at the same time exciting to be with somebody who was so very pleasant. As she continued to walk and talk with Jim, Tanya noticed that the shadows from the trees seemed to be longer than they were before, and a quick glance at her watch shocked her. Tanya couldn't believe what time it was. She was in danger of being late for an important meeting at work. Tanya hurriedly explained this to Jim as she said good-bye to him and ran toward her car. Jim called after her that he'd phone her around 6:30 to firm up plans for going to the Duran Duran reunion concert at Chastain Park on Saturday. As Tanya dodged puddles and crunched leaves on her way to her car, she wondered where the time had gone. Some minutes later she wished she could borrow back some of the time she had lost during the afternoon, because, to Tanya's chagrin, she now found herself stuck in the infamous Atlanta traffic. Even though she only had to go a few miles, traffic was snarled and moving slowly. She glanced at the clock on her dashboard and the digitally displayed numbers seemed to be changing more rapidly than they should; there was no doubt about it, Tanya was going to be late for the meeting. Stopped in traffic, Tanya tapped her foot on the floor in synch with the beat of her hands on the steering wheel as the minutes whizzed by.

Tanya finally made it to the meeting and to her relief no one seemed to be very upset with her late arrival. The meeting, however, was a boring disaster. Tanya sat and marked the slow passage of time by doodling and drawing Jim's name several ways, first by squares and then by triangles and then by long elegant lines and curves. She often looked at her watch, a beautiful gold oval given to her as a graduation gift, and even tapped it a couple of times to be sure that it was still running. Finally, after what seemed like hours (but was actually closer to forty-five minutes), the meeting was over and Tanya was able to make her farewells to her coworkers and head home.

Traffic was again a problem for Tanya as she made her way home but she solved it by going through backstreets and taking shortcuts she had learned in the three years she had lived and worked in Atlanta. She remembered that Jim had said he would call around 6:30, and hoped she would make it home in time. As she turned the corner to reach her favorite shortcut through a tree-lined residential neighborhood, the hands on her wristwatch, which had appeared to be stopped at work, now seemed to be spinning rapidly around. She arrived at her apartment complex and drove into the parking spot assigned to her, walked up the flight of stairs to her second-story apartment, opened the door, and breathed a sigh of relief. She was home.

Tanya's relief was short-lived, however, as she saw what a mess home was. She went from one room to another picking up discarded clothing and putting it in the hamper, and placed leftover dishes from breakfast into the dishwasher. The minutes seemed to go by ever so slowly. She looked again at the clock that sat at her bedside table: 6:25! How could it be 6:25? Had she only been home five minutes? It seemed like a half-hour or so at least. She started at what sounded like a phone ringing; it was, but in the apartment next to her. Damn this place and its thin walls. She was going to have to look for a new apartment that would give her some privacy. Maybe Jim would like to help her find a place. He was so good at getting things done. Maybe when he called she could bring that up as an idea for Sunday. It would be nice to take a ride around, look at apartments, perhaps get something to eat.

Then the phone rang. It was Jim. And time speeded up once again for Tanya.

One very specific way that rhythm affects our lives and social relations is through time. Time is all around us, moving along at the same orderly pace day in and day out. It is the same time here at your house as it is across the street or across town. In fact, you can quickly find out exactly what time it is anywhere else in the world if you want to. You testify daily to your acceptance of the regularity of time by the watch you wear, by the calendar you have up on the wall, and by the appointment book you carry with you or have on your desk. However, you may be less aware of the other aspect of time, its more emotional aspect. Time, as you usually deal with it, is not as regular as clockwork, but instead goes in fits and starts. First it goes slower, then faster, pausing then rushing ahead until, like Tanya, you may be exhausted by the end your day, from trying to keep up with all of its many changes in speed.

The study of the way that people perceive and use time is called *chronemics.* The importance of time is reflected by the countless ways in which the word itself has become part of the way we communicate about our relationship with others: "My time is your time." "Can you spare some time for me?" "We don't spend enough time together." "We're having the time of our lives!" "How time flies when you're having fun." "I'll make time for you." "I don't have time for that." "Let's take a timeout." "Time is our friend." "It's party time." "What a timely suggestion." And so on. As part of a class we teach on relationships, our students have helped us generate nearly a thousand different statements in which time is included as a significant word in the communication of emotional meaning. The old adage "time is money" could very well be rewritten to say "time is emotion" or "time is relationship."

A basic way we show how much we value other people is by how much time we allocate to them, and when we're with them, how much of our valuable time we share with them. Its importance is one reason why there are so many rules about time and punctuality within our culture. A sure way to lose a chance at a job is to be late for a scheduled interview. In contrast, a sure way to lose a friend in New York is to show up at 7:00 P.M. for their party, which is scheduled on the invitation to begin at 7:00 P.M. As Burgoon and Saine, prolific researchers of nonverbal communication, point out in their book on nonverbal behavior, the politically correct late arrival to social events in large eastern cities would be considered rude both in western cities like Salt Lake City and Portland and in most small cities and towns in our country, where the time stated on the invitation is the time you should arrive.

The meaning and use of time not only varies from one area of the country to another, but from one culture to another as well. In their interesting book on cross-cultural behavior, Edward and Mildred Hall have described American culture as operating according to *monochronic* time. Monochronic time is used and experienced linearly, like a road that originates in the past and extends to the future and can be divided easily into segments or compartments. The perception of time as functioning monochronically facilitates our habit of concentrating on one thing at a time. From this perspective, our schedule becomes crucially important and must be followed at all costs. The weekly business meeting must take place at the scheduled time—to change it to another day or another time would be unthinkable.

Hall and Hall go on to point out that monochronic time is perceived as almost tangible and as having the same value as money to be spent, saved, wasted, or lost. They conclude that "because monochronic time concentrates on one thing at a time, people who are governed by it don't like to be interrupted. Monochronic time seals people off from one another and, as a result, intensifies some relationships while shortchanging others. Time becomes a room which some people are allowed to enter, while others are excluded." Monochronic time perspective is not a biological given but rather a vestige of the industrial revolution, when workers had to be in place by appointed times so work could be completed. Some cultures within our own country, such as the Navajo Nation, do not now nor ever have followed monochronic time. The monochronic time perspective only seems natural and logical to most of us because we have been raised according to its rules for all of our lives. It also explains why we follow its tenets even when they may produce illogical and negative results. Why else would we tolerate the horrendous rush hours dictated by a slavish adherence to monochronic time rules, which demand that everybody must report to and leave work at the same designated time?

In contrast to the monochronic time perspective, which segments events and relationships, *polychronic time,* according to Hall and Hall, "is characterized by the simultaneous occurrence of many things and great involvement with people." The emphasis of polychronic time is on people instead of an abstract schedule. If engaged in an interesting exchange with one another, those espousing a polychronic perspective are more likely to continue talking and be late for their next appointments rather than break off their social interaction. In fact, in polychronic cultures, appointments mean relatively less and are often changed to accommodate others in the family or in the circle of close friends. According to Hall and Hall, polychronic time is experienced as less tangible and more like a point or place, as opposed to the long road perspective of monochronic time.

Are You More Monochronic or Polychronic in Your Time Perspective?

Monochronic People	*Polychronic People*
1. Do one thing at a time	Prefer to do many things at one time
2. Stay focused on the task at hand	Tend to be distractible and interruptable
3. Take all time commitments seriously	See time commitments as something to honor if possible
4. Committed to the job at hand	Committed to people and relationships
5. Stick to plans	Change plans often and easily
6. Concerned about privacy	Concerned more about close relationships
7. Great respect for private property	Will borrow and lend often and easily
8. Emphasize promptness	Promptness plays second fiddle to relationships
9. Used to short-term relationships	Tend to build long-term relationships
10. Business before pleasure	Pleasure before business

If they both are unaware that there is more than one way to perceive time, monochronic and polychronic individuals can have difficulty interacting with one another comfortably. Hall and Hall give a clear example of this in the following excerpt.

> A French salesman working for a French company that had recently been bought by Americans found himself with a new American manager who expected instant results and higher profits immediately. Because of the emphasis on personal relationships, it frequently takes years to develop customers in polychronic France, and, in family-owned firms, relationships with customers may span generations. The American manager, not understanding this, ordered the salesman to develop new customers within three months. The salesman knew this was impossible and had to resign, asserting his legal right to take with him all the loyal customers he had developed over the years. Neither side understood what had happened.

When you think about it within the primarily monochronic American culture, our allocation of time carries important relationship meanings. If we misread time cues or express them inappropriately, we can create major problems in our social interactions. *Receptive time dyssemics* make mistakes in reading the time messages sent by others. We can give you a personally painful example of what can result from being dyssemic regarding time.

Receptive Time Dyssemia—Frank

We were at a university lecture. Although the speaker was an internationally renowned researcher, it turned out that he was one of the most boring people you would ever want to hear. He appeared to be as bored by us as we were by him. It was clear that he wanted to leave as quickly after his talk as he could, and most of the audience appeared to be in full agreement. After he finished his talk and the polite applause was over, he asked if there were any questions. As he finished, he first stared intently at his watch and then began to pull his papers together to put in his briefcase—both nonverbal messages that clearly communicated that he did not want to spend any more time with us. The audience got the message and we all began to gather our own belongings to leave when, to our collective horror, a hand went up and waved vigorously. It was Frank. Frank is a receptive time dyssemic who doesn't have a clue about reading time-related nonverbal messages, such as those sent by our speaker. He proceeded to ask not one but a series of questions, oblivious to the irritation communicated by the audience's shuffling feet and the speaker's frowning face and brief answers.

Whom we choose to spend our time with and how much of our time we decide to allocate to them are powerful interpersonal messages. As with Frank in the story above, receptive time dyssemics have trouble understanding the meaning of time cues sent by others. They don't read, for example, the intended negative information implicit in others' continual refusals to spend time with them. They don't realize that they have been sent negative messages when they get five minutes with someone instead of the hour they asked for, or a quick cup of coffee instead of the luncheon meeting they had requested. Receptive time dyssemics have not learned to read the cues in such expressions of time and may often, in these instances, believe they have a much closer relationship with someone than they actually do. The meanings of many expressions of time have to be learned, like the institutionalized academic rules that say students should wait five minutes for an assistant professor, ten minutes for an associate professor, and fifteen minutes for a full professor to arrive before assuming a class is cancelled. Sensitivity to the meaning of time messages is a subtle yet important social skill. Whether working, playing, eating, or talking with others, you must be able to read their time cues so that you know whether or not you've spent enough time with them in this or that activity and should move on to something else.

Expressive time dyssemics are the flip side of this problem. Instead of having trouble reading the time cues of others, these people have an equal difficulty expressing time cues appropriately. For example, expressive time dyssemics are unaware of the fact that by repeatedly keeping other people waiting, they are communicating that they are uncaring, self-centered, and/or irresponsible. Punctuality is valued in our society. If you have an appointment on the other side of town at 6:00 P.M., then you are expected to put in the extra time and effort required to be certain you'll be there on time. This means you might have to (1) allow more time for the trip than you usually do, because there may be extra traffic at rush hour; (2) scout for other routes in case one way or the other is blocked; and/or (3) make sure the car has gasoline so time won't be wasted stopping to fill up on the way. In our society, to show up on time says that you really do care about an individual; to be late means just the opposite.

Most people in our monochronic society see time management as a reflection of one's intelligence and caring for others. Are you dyssemic for time usage? Answer the questions in sidebar and find out.

Are You Dyssemic for Time Usage?

- Are you often late for work?
- Are you often late for eating out with friends?
- Are you often late for meetings?
- Are you frequently too early for work?
- Are you frequently too early for meetings?
- Do you find yourself making excuses to others about why you're late?
- Are you late with handing in assignments where you work?
- Are you usually late paying your bills?
- Are you late with getting your taxes in?
- Have you ever run out of gasoline?

If you answer three or more of the questions "yes," there is a possibility that you may be dyssemic in reading the demands of time. The higher the score, the greater the likelihood that you are dyssemic in this area.

If it turns out that you are dyssemic for time usage, then some practice in time management may be called for. A time-management program includes making you much more aware of time and its passing by keeping extensive time records. While we will go into greater detail on this in later chapters, one easy way to help increase your sensitivity to time is to practice estimating its passage. Just sit and see if you can guess how long it takes for thirty seconds to pass, or one minute or maybe even five. Another way to lay the foundation for managing time is to make an activities schedule beginning with getting up in the morning and ending with going to bed. On this list, estimate the amount of time it takes to accomplish these everyday activities. For example, next to "eating breakfast," put thirty minutes if that is how long it takes you. Do this for each activity of the day until you have accounted for all the ways you spend your time. Next, record exactly how much time it actually does take you to complete these activities. When that is recorded, put down the amount of time you would like to spend doing each activity and note the significant differences. These will be your key focus areas where you will make conscious efforts to change. This activity may be enough to help sensitize you to your use of time and how you can make yourself more time astute.

Let us make one final comment about time. There is public time that is shared with others, and there is also private time that you reserve for yourself and your own private thoughts, dreams, wishes, and fantasies. Most of what is written about time involves the use of public time, where we share our experiences and communications with others. School, company parties, and family picnics are examples of public time where we enjoy the give-and-take of communication with others. We agree that these are critically important for being with others and for learning how to be in proper relationship with them. We also believe that not enough time is given over to private reverie and to paying attention to our own thoughts and feelings. A number of formal programs (such as those in Yoga and mediation) are available to help you learn to clarify and organize your thoughts; however, we don't think you need formal training to become adept at spending time with yourself. We ask you to give yourself the gift of a quiet place to spend time with your own thoughts for about a half-hour once or twice a week. Through private times like these, not only will you feel better about yourself but you also will become more sensitive to the communications of others in your more public times. You deserve and need these private times.

Personal Space

Personal space is like a bubble that surrounds us and comes with us wherever we go, contracting and expanding depending on the situation we are in. Personal space can be differentiated from *territorial space* to which we feel connected because of our ownership or identification. We are territorial about where we live, especially our homes and our cars. Should someone come close to or on to our "turf" uninvited, we become vigilant and tense as to his or her purpose. We hate tailgaters and we find it hard to tolerate someone in another car looking at us. As comedian George Carlin has quipped, we even feel disquieted if someone is driving next to us at our speed! Many of our favorite team sports, such as football, basketball, and soccer, are based on the idea of defending territory.

While territorial space is important to us, it is not as relevant to our ongoing daily interactions as is our personal space. Because space is always present and we are always in space or moving through space, we tend to forget it is there. Personal space usually acts as background to whatever else might be going on in our foreground and, as a result, it easily disappears from our awareness—that is, until somebody invades what we consider to be our own personal space, and then we become very much aware of it and how important it is to us. This is clearly illustrated in situations where we find ourselves crowded together with strangers in a small space, like an elevator.

The Importance of Space: Elton in the Elevator

Elton was going to see his lawyer. As he stood on the first floor of the vast office building, looking at his reflection in the newly polished floor while waiting for the elevator to come, he was aware of the fact that he was not looking forward to this meeting. After all, how much fun was it going to be to see someone about making up a will. But he supposed he was at an age when it was time to talk to someone about such matters.

The elevator finally arrived and Elton got in, pushed the button for his floor, ambled over to the back left corner, leaned against the wall in a semi-slouch, and continued to think about his life and his health. It wasn't long, however, before the elevator stopped and the door opened to let in another rider. Although he didn't really get a clear look at the person, Elton responded to the arrival of a new rider by immediately straightening his posture, clearing his throat, and putting his arms at his sides. The other passenger, a man a few years younger than Elton, said "Excuse me" as he leaned in front of him to push a button for his floor, after which he walked over to the far corner of the elevator. He sort of stood at attention as well and directed his gaze away from Elton. If one were to measure the distance between Elton and his new elevator peer, the results would reveal that they were standing as far away from each another as possible. As the elevator continued its ascent, other passengers joined them and they too took places equidistant from one another so that the available space was being used as judiciously as it could be. But nothing could prevent the elevator from filling up with more people and soon it was difficult for anyone to have anything approaching a comfortable amount of personal space. It was at this point that Elton awoke from his reverie about the briefness of life and all of its many trials and made some interesting observations about his fellow passengers.

With the elevator full of riders, all of whom were strangers to one another, he noted that no one was looking at anyone else. In fact, all the passengers seemed to be behaving in generally the same way: they all had their heads tilted upward, their mouths slightly open, and their eyes gazing up at the changing numbers above the door, lighting up for the different floors passing by. Then something strange happened. One of the men who was looking up at the numbers moved his head slightly to the left and looked at the man next to him. Immediately, the man to his left swung his head around quickly and with an angry facial expression and tone of voice said, "You got a problem, mister?" The man who had initiated the unfortunate look was very embarrassed, as were Elton and the rest of the passengers, and he apologized profusely. In fact, after apologizing, he got off at the next floor even though Elton was sure he had not pushed that floor number when he had first gotten on the elevator. After the doors closed, the passengers again returned their gaze to the numbers and resumed their zombielike state. Although Elton found this interesting, he soon forgot about it as the bell sounded and the doors opened for the floor where his lawyer's office was located. After all, he had wills and his own mortality to think about.

What happened in the elevator was almost completely determined by the rules that exist for the use of personal space. Wherever we go during our waking hours, we carry our bubble of personal space, which if made visible would be seen to extend around us in all directions, going out further on our sides and back than it does in front. The greater distance toward the rear is there to protect us from dangers we cannot see and thereby cannot anticipate as well as we can those that approach us from the front. Our egg-shaped bubble of personal space accompanies us into every one of our interactions and determines how far away we stand or sit from other people.

Even if we can't actually see the personal space bubbles surrounding us and others, we can see their effects by watching two acquaintances approach one another from opposite directions. If we watch them closely, we will see that they will acknowledge one another with a wave when they are about fifteen to twenty feet apart. Then, when the distance between them closes to about twelve feet, we will see them begin to slow down the pace of their approach. The pace will continue to slow until they are about four feet away from each other. Four feet is about the distance most of us (at least in the United States) feel is a comfortable distance for speaking to another person who is an acquaintance. If we continue to watch the acquaintances closely, we will see them both take a small step or two backward or forward as they reach this four-foot distance. This rocking motion occurs because they have "hit" one another's personal space bubble. The steps they took after they hit were part of the final negotiation over the proper comfortable distance between them, at which their conversation can take place.

The conversational space these two acquaintances settled on is called the *personal zone,* a term coined by Edward T. Hall, a leading contributor to the understanding of personal space. According to Hall there are not one but actually four distinct space zones, each of them appropriate for certain types of conversational content. (See the illustration that shows the four zones Hall suggests are used in the United States). The zone closest to us is called the *intimate zone,* and it extends from just off our skin to a distance of about a foot and a half away. In this zone it is proper to discuss intimate and important topics or to converse about most anything with someone with whom we are very deeply involved. We have all told secrets in our time and can remember how we cupped our hands over our mouths so that others could not hear the important information we were passing along to our confidant. Likewise, we have all seen romantic couples sitting or standing very close to one another, talking with high intensity and completely oblivious to those around them. The short distance makes it very difficult if not impossible for anyone but the involved parties to hear what is being said. It is considered the height of rudeness to listen in to a conversation going on within this intimate zone. Perhaps that is one reason why people talking on cell phones make us so uncomfortable—we are privy to what is supposed to be conversation taking place in the intimate zone.

When we are less than eighteen inches from another human being, other nonverbal channels of communication often come into play that are consistent with the intimacy of the zone. For

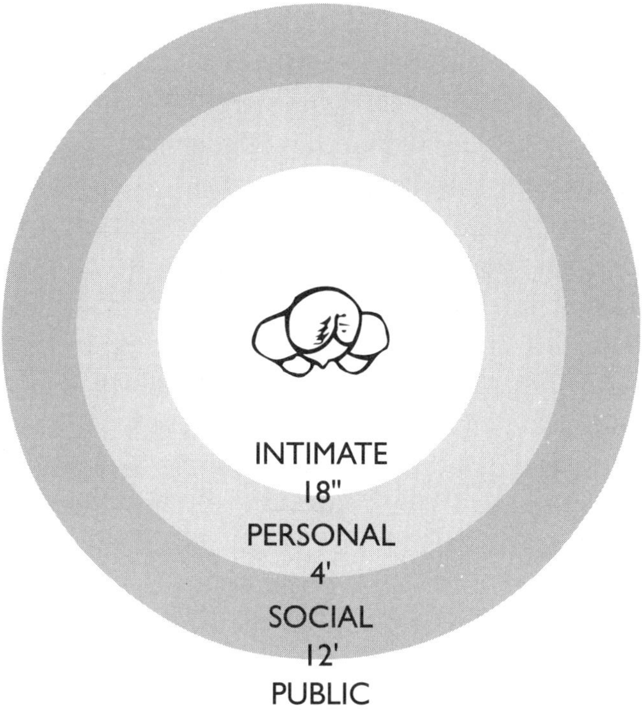

Zones of personal space

example, within the intimate zone it is possible to smell whatever scents are being carried on one anothers' bodies and to feel and smell one anothers' breath during conversation. Of course, if we are only eighteen inches or less from another person it facilitates the possibility that touch can occur, which, in turn, can further increase the intimacy of the interaction. It makes us and those around us very uncomfortable when others with whom we are not intimate enter this space, with its implications of intimacy, and we usually will take steps—both literally and figuratively—to create more distance. You may remember that one of Kyle's many nonverbal errors involved standing too close to others.

Many of us have had the occasion to be disconcerted by observing someone close to us interacting with someone else within this intimate zone. If, for instance, you should happen to see your spouse or your boy or girlfriend across the room in animated conversation with an eligible other person, and that conversation is taking place within the eighteen-inch space, our bet is that it wouldn't be long before you ambled over to see for yourself what exactly is going on.

The intimate zone is reserved for only a select few. Most of our important interpersonal interactions take place in the *personal zone.* This zone extends from about eighteen inches to around four feet. It was at around four feet that the two approaching acquaintances described above stopped to have their conversation, and it is the distance that most of us will choose to converse with others as well. This is the distance that allows us to talk without straining our voices. This is the distance at which we can speak in our normal voice rather than whispering (as we might do in the intimate range) or shouting (as we might do in the social or public distance ranges). Restaurant tables, for example, are usually set up for individuals to sit between eighteen inches and four feet apart. If you want a more intimate dining experience, you can sit so that your elbows rest on the table and reduce the distance by half, or you can sit side by side rather than across from one another. When you are seated at a larger table for a meal, you will talk most with those individuals with whom you have eye contact and who are within a four-foot radius of where you are seated.

How to Heighten Awareness of Personal Space if You Suspect You Are Dyssemic

Here are a few activities you can engage in that will help you become more sensitive to the personal space around you. Try one or more of them when you have a chance.

- Go to a public setting like a shopping mall, sporting event, outside restaurant, or coffee shop, and watch the people walking around. Try to guess what the relationship is between individuals by observing how close they stand or sit next to one another.
- Observe people who are in conversation with one another. Note how far they stand away from one another. Is it at the four-foot personal zone or the closer intimate zone? If it is two men, see if they adopt the "V" stance, where they are not looking at one another but are standing at an angle to one another as though they were looking at something in the distance.
- Break a few personal-space rules (just for learning purposes) and see what happens. For example, walk between two people having a conversation in the personal zone or get in an elevator and rather than stand on the other side of the car, stand next to the person already in the car. See how uncomfortable you and others involved feel.
- Attend a church, synagogue, or mosque. Note how people choose where to sit. Do the middle or the ends of the rows fill up first? How about the seats at the front or the back of the hall?

Beyond the personal zone lies the *social zone,* which extends from four to about twelve feet. While social interaction is permitted in this zone, it lacks the privacy of the intimate and personal zones. In fact, it is appropriate to talk loud enough when you are in this zone for others to overhear what you are saying. If you are approaching someone from some distance, you might feel comfortable shouting hello when you are about twelve feet away. Because others have access to what is communicated in the social zone, it is not appropriate to discuss intimate or personal matters there.

The final space demarcation is the largest of Hall's four categories and is called the *public zone.* It begins at the end of social space, at about twelve feet, and extends to infinity. Typically, communication in this zone is not characterized by talking except in special instances, such as public events like speeches or lectures. In such instances, speech primarily travels one way: from the speaker to the audience. If the audience is going to communicate back it most likely will have to use the long-distance channels of postures and gestures (see chapter 5).

The rules governing what is to be talked about at what interpersonal distance are very stringent. Parker got himself in relationship difficulties because of his inability to follow these rules.

Being Dyssemic for Personal Space—Parker

Parker liked to think of himself as just a really great guy. He was always ready to meet people and to find out more about them, and was genuinely interested in what they did and what they thought about things. He prided himself on his ability to walk up to anyone, no matter who they were, and start a conversation. Parker worked in the office of the history department of a large university in the northwestern United States. One of his responsibilities was to greet visitors, primarily students, who came to the department office. Parker was hired because of his easy manner and the seeming openness of his interactive style. However, unbeknownst to his superiors and to Parker himself, he actually was a terrible choice for this job because he lacked both knowledge about and skill in using personal space.

Early one morning, a very nervous-looking student tentatively came through the door that opened into the history department office, looked around anxiously, and slowly approached Parker's desk, which was about ten feet from the door. "Excuse me," she said, almost in a whisper. "Can I please speak to Dr. Mabinnee?"

"Sure," Parker replied, "I'm pretty sure he's in. Let's see, I think his office is in Room 212." Then, rather than give verbal directions, Parker got up out of his chair and stood about ten inches from the girl's face as he pointed her down the hall to Dr. Mabinnee's office. In response to this inappropriate intimacy, the student's face turned a bright beet red and she quickly pulled away from Parker and hurriedly left the office. Parker noticed none of this and merely congratulated himself on being so personable.

Later that same afternoon, Parker was in the office with two other office staff members and three others who were involved in other department business. The office was a fairly large one for an academic institution, because history was a very popular major at this university. Parker's office workmates sat between fifteen and twenty feet away from him. Parker was busily putting the class schedules in order when he remembered that one of his coworkers, Doris, had been out recently with stomach flu and he had forgotten to ask her how she was doing. Doris was sitting with a student explaining scheduling choices when she heard Parker shout from the other side of the room, "How's the diarrhea, Doris? Did you finally get something that stopped you up?" All eyes in the office suddenly turned toward Doris and she felt like a very bright spotlight had been turned on her. She turned to the student with whom she had been working with a bewildered expression on her face and then said hurriedly, before Parker could shout anything more, "I'm fine. Thanks for asking. I'll talk to you later." Parker said, "Sure thing," and went back to his work, whistling one of his favorite songs.

Parker is a perfect example of someone who is unaware of breaking the content-of-conversation and space rule. In the first instance, he inappropriately moved into the intimate space zone to talk about a social or public topic with someone who was a stranger to him. As so often happens with expressive dyssemics such as Parker, they are also receptively dyssemic and fail to read the nonverbal responses others give to their inappropriate behavior. Parker did not notice the anxiousness of the student when she came in, nor the cues of discomfort and embarrassment sent by her facial expressions when he invaded her personal space. In fact, Parker had just the opposite response to his interaction with her: He thought he did just fine. In the second instance, Parker violated the rule that you do not talk about intimate-zone topics in social or public space. Though he was trying to show concern, his shouting across the office the question about Doris's diarrhea let everyone know some information that Doris would have preferred to keep to herself.

Although most of us learn what we need to know about space usage during our childhood, there are some of us who don't, and end up either receptive or expressively dyssemic for using space. Such was the case of Allison.

Dyssemia for Space in Certain Contexts—Allison

Allison was a nice person who didn't have a clue about space usage. In her early thirties, she was an only child who lived at home with her parents, who had absolutely adored her as a child and continued to adore her as an adult. She was tall and thin and attractive in her own way, and had held a job as an assistant teller at the local credit union for nearly a decade, although her time there had not been without problems. She was a conscientious and hardworking woman who did her job well and was liked by her customers, but Allison was seen as strange by most everyone else. One of the major reasons for the disparity between the positive feelings of her customers and the negative feelings of others was her lack of skill in using personal space. When she worked, Allison sat behind a large marble counter, in an area that was structured and immovable. The space between Allison and her customers was held constant by this heavy slab of marble. There she sat on her tall stool every day and greeted each customer that came to her window with a big smile and a warm greeting. Her customers were well satisfied with this pleasant, efficient woman. In fact, some customers liked her so much they would even wait in her line for service even when other lines were shorter. However, that was not the way that her coworkers felt about Allison.

Allison's problems began the minute she got off her teller's stool and left the safe, structured confines of her workstation. First, there were the problems with men. Allison had complained to her superiors about being harassed by the men around her. The men in return said that Allison led them on by standing too close to them and not rebuffing them when they responded by standing equally close to her. Allison didn't understand any of this. She was not aware of standing too close to men and certainly couldn't tell when they were standing too close to her. Allison didn't understand the emotional meaning of space or how to read or express herself spatially.

Allison had difficulties with women as well because, they said, they did not know what to expect from her. Sometimes she would openly discuss intimate topics in a loud voice that most everyone in the break room could hear. Then there was her habit of walking right between two people who were talking to one another in the hall to get to the Coke machine, without giving a "please," "excuse me," or "sorry." She had done this sort of thing to most everyone at work and they were all absolutely furious with her. How could she seem so nice at one moment and then be so rude the next? Because they didn't know what to make of her, they just stayed away. As a result, Allison had few friends and fewer dates. She despondently felt like she would never live away from home and would be at the same teller window doing the same things for the rest of her life.

Although children are allowed to break more space rules than adults, we expect individuals to use space accurately from about ten years of age and older. We have little patience or time with space-rule violators. As we pointed out in the movie theater example in the introduction, if you are someone who breaks the rules of space usage, you stand a good chance of being feared, shunned, and rejected by others.

People like Allison and Parker, who constantly break residual rules of personal-space usage, have not learned what they need to know to make relationships work well. They need to acquire the personal-space skills they lack by first being made aware that they have a problem in using personal space and then by being taught directly what the four zones of personal space are and what is appropriate within each of them. One obvious way to do this is to make personal space more visible and concrete to them. In young children, this has easily been done by having them wear hula hoops for a day or so. This helps to make the distance they should stand away from one another concrete and observable. It turns out that each hula hoop creates about two feet of distance, so two hula hoops touching produce the appropriate distance for conversation.

Adults cannot walk around with hula hoops at work (although what you do in the privacy of your own home is your business). More likely, adults could become more knowledgeable and aware of personal space by reading about it and then completing the exercises suggested in this and later chapters. Experiences like dancing, exercise with movement, or Yoga practices that include learning about how your body moves through space would be helpful.

One final note about space usage: The zones of personal space we have described in this chapter are appropriate for the United States. It is important to realize that zones of personal space are learned and may differ from culture to culture. What might be the appropriate distance to discuss a particular topic in Saudi Arabia may be very different from the correct distance in the United States. Remember this when you are interacting with someone from another country or traveling abroad.

We mentioned at the start of this chapter that rhythm, time, and personal space are especially important because of their box four status as behavior that we rarely attend to. In their diffuse way, they set the background for our interpersonal interactions. Without using them properly, we may never get to interact for very long with anyone. But when we do, another set of nonverbal behaviors becomes important. We now turn to the nonverbal behaviors that provide the lion's share of information when we interact with others: facial expressions and paralanguage.

Chapter 4

Channels of Nonverbal Behavior: Faces and Voices

Unlike rhythm, time, and considerations of personal space, which usually operate well beyond our ability to see them even when we are aware of their existence (box four), we usually are more aware of facial expressions and paralanguage. You probably don't need to be convinced that facial expressions and paralanguage are intimately involved in your day-to-day social interactions. Both Kyle and Amy, the two people whom you met at the start of this book, had trouble with one or the other of them. However, although most people might acknowledge the importance of facial expressions and tones of voice, most of us probably have little idea how adept we are at using them, and a surprising proportion of us are dyssemic in their use.

While personal space, rhythm, and time are certainly important in any nonverbal language vocabulary, we are sure that no one has ever said to you in the heat of an emotional discussion, "Look me straight in my space bubble!" When push comes to shove, if we want to know how people are feeling, we lock on to their faces and voices and use what we see and hear there. And this is not just folk wisdom. Ample clinical experience and research points clearly to the fact that facial expressions and paralanguage are centrally important. One of our students once told us about his grandmother, who used to say to him, "Don't look at me with that tone of voice!" What his grandma knew is that there is great power in the facial expressions that we produce and in the way in which we "color" the words we use with variations in pitch and loudness. In this chapter, we are going to tell you first about some of the ways that facial expressions are involved in the relationship process. We then will turn to paralanguage, the component of nonverbal language that accounts for more of the emotional impact we have on others than any other single channel. If you are going to succeed in interacting with others, you must be able to use these two modes of communication adequately.

Facial Expressions

We are all aware of faces and how they look. In United States culture, when we meet people we aren't supposed to look at their elbows or knees or past them into space, we are supposed to gaze at their face. We do so for a reason: because looking at others' faces gives us valuable clues about how they are feeling and thinking. But looks can sometimes be deceiving.

The Resting Face—Sylvia

Sylvia had decided that she wanted to be a psychotherapist. She was a bright, attractive, twenty-five-year-old woman who had always wanted to help others. As a child, Sylvia would play pretend games with her friends in which she was always the kindly nurse or friendly teacher who helped make other peoples' problems get better. After graduating, Sylvia volunteered for VISTA (Volunteers in Service to America) and spent two years teaching at-risk children in inner-city settings. During her Teach America tenure, Sylvia decided that she wanted to be a clinical psychologist. Because of her excellent academic record and letters of recommendation, she received a number of invitations to interview at university programs in clinical psychology and schools of professional psychology. Things hadn't gone well at her early interviews. In fact, approaching her final program interview, she felt as though if she didn't make a good impression here, she wouldn't get in anywhere.

It was the final interview at the end of a long day of meeting professors and students, and Sylvia was sitting in the chairperson's office wondering if her dream of becoming a psychotherapist was about to be crushed. Janet, the chair, sat down, opened Sylvia's folder, and took a moment to look through it. Then she put the folder down and said, "I've never done this with any other applicant, but Frans, your undergraduate adviser, is a good friend of mine and he told me your interviews weren't going well. Sylvia, I think I know why they're not going well and if you will give me permission to give you my opinion, I'd like to share it with you."

Sylvia squared her shoulders and said to Janet, "Yes, I'd really like to know what's going on."

"Sylvia, you are a marvelous student, but when we choose among the applicants for positions in our program we have only a few minutes to form impressions and make judgments. Frankly, your facial expression is confusing! You look like you are either angry or bored. I've talked with my colleagues and they have the impression that you really don't want to come to our program. Is that true?"

Sylvia was shocked. It took her a moment or two to compose herself and respond that she would love to be part of this program. She confessed that she had never thought about what her facial expressions were like.

Janet looked straight at Sylvia and said, "I'm going to take a chance on you. I like the way you've responded to this tough feedback. If you'll promise me that you will work on your facial expressions, especially those when you are just listening to someone else talking, I'll recommend you for our program." Sylvia couldn't believe her ears and smiled brightly. "There," Janet said, "that's a whole different you that is being shown through that smile. Now that you know what was getting in the way, you can work on it and you will be just fine."

Sylvia is dyssemic in the most basic of the facial expressions, the "resting face." The resting face is the expression you show when you are in "neutral" emotionally. About 75 percent of people have a resting face that is either neutral or positive in emotional tone. Close to 25 percent have a resting face that may be interpreted as negative. That is, even when you are feeling nothing in particular, your facial expression is communicating that you are feeling something negative, such as fear, anger, or sadness. To get an idea of what we're talking about, look at the illustration of some positive and negative resting faces.

A negative resting face, you may remember, was the problem for Amy, the expressive dyssemic we described to you in the introduction. By contrast, many interpersonally successful people appear to have a slightly positive "tone" to their resting face. They look content, even moderately happy—even when they are not. The impact of such a positive resting face can be seen in places such as school cafeterias or office lunchrooms. People looking for someone to just sit with are far more likely to approach someone with a positive than a negative resting face.

Sylvia was having just the opposite effect with her hostile-appearing resting face. While she thought she was communicating respect and interest while she listened to and interacted with students and faculty of the schools where she was interviewing, Sylvia was giving the impression of begin arrogant and irritated. No wonder she didn't get chosen to be a student in these programs.

There are a number of ways that you can tell whether you have a problem resting face. People might often ask you questions like, "Are you all right?" or "Is something wrong?" when you are feeling perfectly fine. In any place where there is public seating, are you one of the last who others will sit next to? Are you not included in conversations? Next time, pay attention to the way others approach you when you are sitting alone at lunch or on a coffee break. Feedback from others will tell you if you are one of the who exhibits a bad resting facial expression.

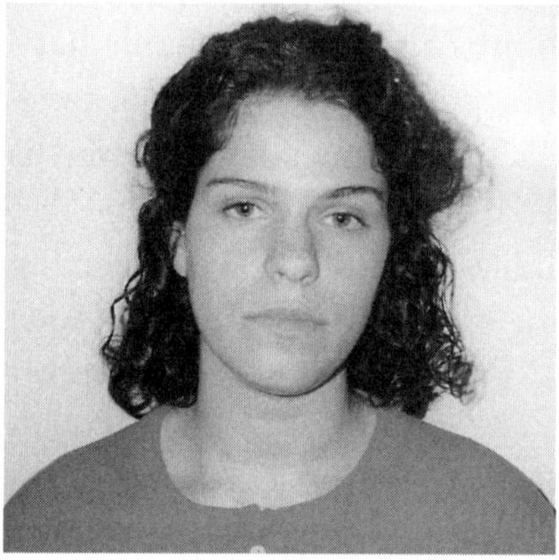

A

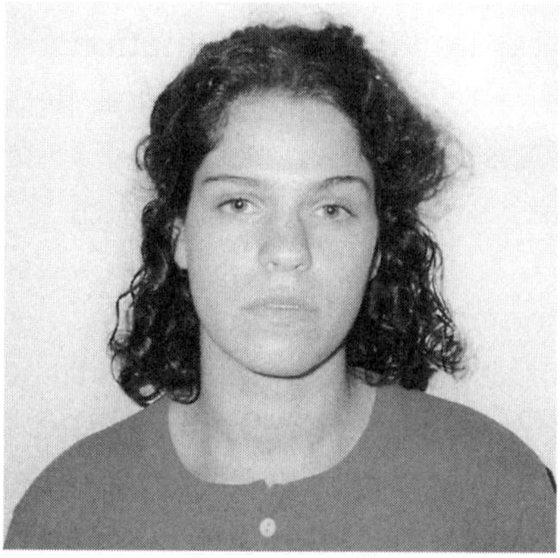

B

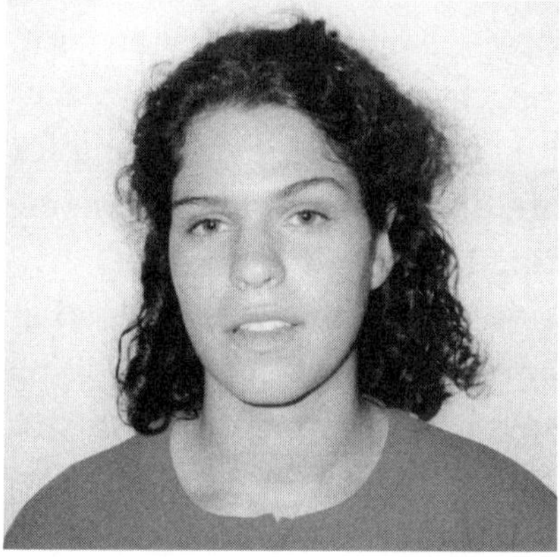

C

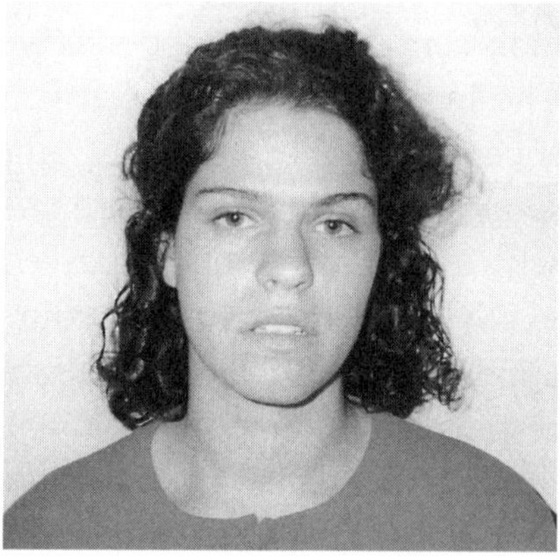

D

E

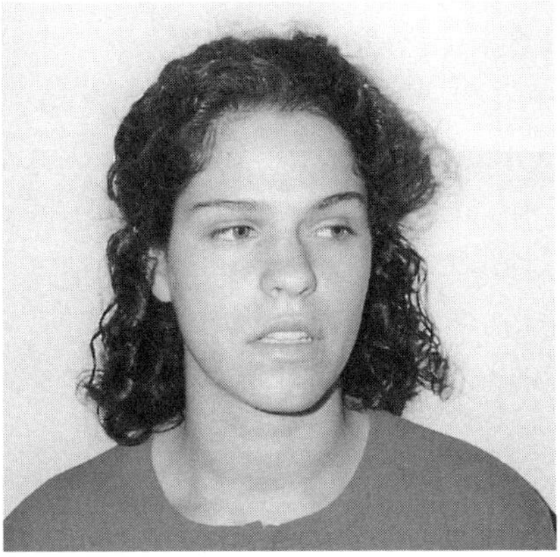

F

Resting faces can have a significant effect on how people respond to us. Look at the photos above. Notice first that they vary in intensity, with those at the top much more difficult to "read" than those below. Compare the photos on the right with those on the left. In each pair, the right-hand photo is negative, while the left is more positive. Though this contrast is easy to see in pairs CD and EF, it is more elusive in pair AB. However, people can and do respond to even the slight negativity of a resting face, such as seen in photo B. Have your coach take some "neutral" photos of your facial expression. Can you detect a slight positive? Good! If you discern a slight negative, work on it!

Our resting face is especially important in determining how the *choice* and *beginning stages* of interpersonal relationships go. Recall that it is in this stage that people select someone to talk to. If we're not selected, we'll have no conversation. If we have no conversation—no first date. No first date—no relationship development. No relationship development—no deepening. No deepening—no permanence. We think you get the idea. As one of our past professors once reminded us, "We marry people who were once total strangers to us."

Before we leave the topic of the resting face, we want to warn you of one further consideration. As we age, our face loses its elasticity and begins to "fall." One result of the aging process is that as we become older, we have an increasing likelihood of developing a negative resting face, even though we may previously have had a positive one. The sad fact is that nearly two of four adults past the age of fifty may experience interpersonal limits because they have a negative resting face and don't know it. Negative resting faces are one reason why grandparents may unintentionally frighten their grandchildren when they put their faces too close, too soon. If you're over fifty, it would be a good idea to look at some photographs and see if you have developed a negative resting face.

Expressive Dyssemia in Facial Communication—Ken

Ken is a thirty-nine-year-old administrative assistant to the director of one of the major national collegiate football bowl games. Ken played football in college and majored in journalism. When he graduated, he found a job with a dot-com company, writing sports copy for their website. He found this interesting for a time, but when the opportunity arose to work for the bowl, he interviewed for and got the job. The fact that he knew football and could write about it well contributed to the decision to hire him. Luckily, his relationship skills were not critical to this entry-level position as publicity and news-release writer.

About a year after he started, the director left unexpectedly and Ken was asked to step in temporarily. Suddenly, he was thrust into a situation where he did not spend most of his day before a computer screen and printer. He was very excited at the thought of working with big-time college players, coaches, and athletic directors, but he was not ready for the social/interpersonal demands that he faced. Very quickly, he began to experience stress and anxiety at work and his performance suffered. Ken heard about the counseling work that we do from one of his coworkers and he got in contact with us.

Ken was as nice a guy as you would want to meet. He spoke with a warm tone of voice and at the drop of a hat would go out of his way to help people. When we met him, however, we were struck by the fact that he possessed the most unexpressive face we had ever seen. Had we had a camera and asked him to make a happy face, then a sad face, then an angry face, then a frightened face, all of the resulting photos would have looked the same!

Imaging the impact of Ken's expressive facial dyssemia on his daily interactions. Not only was he difficult to read, but he was working in a situation where he needed to deal with bowl supporters from the business community, with the press, and with a variety of other people who expected "schmoozing." Our advice to Ken was twofold. First, we felt that he should ask his boss to remove him from his spot as temporary director and allow him to get back to the job that he did well. Second, we outlined a remediation program to help Ken address his facial expressive dyssemia. Ken was very cooperative and motivated in seeing the program through, with the result that he is still working for the bowl and has improved his facial expressiveness significantly.

Although Ken had a remediable expressive dyssemia, there are some individuals whose facial dyssemia is neurologically determined by what is called the Moebius syndrome. We first learned about people with this syndrome when we received an e-mail shortly after the publication of our book *Helping the Child Who Doesn't Fit In*. The writer was the mother of a fourteen-year-old girl—we'll call her Anna—who had Moebius syndrome. In the Moebius syndrome, there is facial paralysis in which, in addition to experiencing eating and swallowing difficulties, victims are unable to smile or frown or move their eyes back and forth in an expressive way. The facial result is a constantly neutral or "droopy" resting face that does not change regardless of what the person is thinking or feeling. Imagine how difficult it would be to interact with someone like Anna, who doesn't change her facial expression.

Not surprisingly, Anna's mother went on to describe how difficult interactions were for her daughter. Other people were uncomfortable in conversations with her and often misinterpreted her feelings and intentions. Once they got to know Anna, they learned to not attend to her facial expressions, but to focus more on her words and her gestures, postures, and voice tone. The future looks brighter for Anna. Her mother reported that her daughter was going to go through plastic surgery to help produce a more positive resting face.

Receptive Facial Dyssemia—Janet

Janet was a forty-eight-year-old school system nutritionist from New Mexico. Never married, Janet had grown up as an only child in a family that was significantly underexpressive. By this we mean that her parents tended not to present many clearly differentiated facial expressions or emotions for her to see. When they were feeling almost anything just moderately, Janet recalled, they seemed to look, as she put it, "pretty bland." In our formal assessment of Janet, we found that she had particular problems differentiating faces depicting low-intensity fear and sadness from those depicting low-intensity anger, and would often mistake one for the other. She was able to easily identify faces expressing high-intensity feelings, but it was when she got to trying to read the more subtle presentations that she began to make mistakes. This problem affected her life in significant ways.

While she was a fine nutritionist and was highly respected and valued by her school system, Janet was a woman with few close friends. Her pattern of living had become one in which she minimized exposure to unstructured situations in which she would need to depend upon accurate interpersonal perception and behavior in order to function well. Without even knowing why, she spent most of her leisure time taking a variety of lessons and attending various clubs (cooking, reading, and travel) where the activities were always organized and dictated. She reported that these were her most comfortable times. The most uncomfortable were typically events where she simply had to talk to people without a predetermined topic.

Janet told us that she had little clue why she had the sorts of relationship problems that had characterized her life, but one thing that had stuck with her was a comment made to her when she was in her thirties by a short-term boyfriend. In giving his reasons for discontinuing their relationship, he had told her that she "always seemed to say the wrong thing at the wrong time." Janet never really understood this, but we told her that we might. The problem was her misinterpretation of other's feelings. The fact is that most of the emotions that we must read in our daily interactions with people are subtle—low intensity. We are taught not to make any strong facial expressions, to raise our voices, or to gesture wildly. We associate these sorts of nonverbal patterns with small children. As we grow, we move, for example, from facially expressing anger by tightening up our faces and glaring with bared teeth to things often as simple and hard to detect as raising one eyebrow a fraction of an inch. People who do not know how to read subtle facial signs are going to be in serious trouble socially. This was Janet's situation. Once we pinned down her problem, she was able to begin a process of remediation and, on a two-year follow-up, she reported that things were going better for her.

Reading facial expressions is something we have to do all day, every day, when we are around people. Difficulties in reading others accurately can make social interaction difficult if not impossible. See sidebar for an exercise to help sensitize you to your ability to read facial expressions.

Reading Facial Expressions

Find one of those ubiquitous posters or T-shirts that ask the question "How are you feeling today?" and provide cartoon characters portraying facial expressions for a variety of emotions. These are meant to be playful (they are now in different languages all over the world!) and fun, but they can be a serious help to you. Look at the faces. Cover the labels under them and see if you can correctly identify them. Do you really see why they reflect their label?

To be able to read and send emotional information accurately is a necessary skill people need in order to be interpersonally competent. As important as facial expressions are, however, they have to take second place to the next channel of nonverbal communication we are going to describe, paralanguage.

The Sounds We Make: Paralanguage

Slow Talkers of America

Have you ever been with someone who talked very slowly? Did they stress you out as you waited for what seemed like an eternity for each word to be spoken? Bob Elliot and Ray Goulding, who made their fame as radio comedians Bob and Ray, developed a classic skit in which Ray, in only a spare few minutes, attempts to interview Bob, who is playing the role of the president of the STOA, the Slow Talkers of America. Bob is patient during the early phases of the interview, but becomes increasingly distressed as his simple questions are answered ever so slowly and carefully by Ray. Soon Ray is filling in the answers to his own questions during the torturously long pauses Bob takes in giving his answers. The skit reaches its peak when, in answer to Ray's question of how many people are attending the STOA convention, Bob first says seven hundred, than, after a few seconds pause—during which Ray begins to talk because he believes Bob is finished—adds "fifty." This throws Ray off and as he begins to apologize for interrupting Bob, Bob adds "three," which completely crushes Ray.

The rate of a person's speech is one component of the single most important channel of nonverbal communication, *paralanguage.* Paralanguage refers to all aspects of sound that accompany words or are independent from words. These aspects of sound include tone of voice, loudness, intensity, and the noises made between words, like humming, whistling, or clearing one's throat.

Research has suggested that nearly one-third of the emotional meaning in conversations is carried by paralanguage, a proportion that increases as visual nonverbal channels are eliminated or lessened in their impact, and reaches its highest impact in conversations taking place over telephones or other nonvisual communication devices. As with the other nonverbal channels, individuals can have both receptive and expressive difficulties in paralanguage.

Receptive Dyssemia in Paralanguage—Markus

Markus was twenty-nine years old and a successful businessman, selling more than any other salesperson with similar experience. As a result of his performance, management gave him a promotion that put Markus in the central office and in charge of over a dozen salespeople's accounts. His future looked very bright. However, at the end of his first year at his new job, it was clear that Markus was failing. It was at that time that his supervisor suggested that Markus come to see us.

We were impressed by what we saw when we met Markus. He was a good-looking, well-groomed, and socially skilled man whom we had no trouble liking. We assessed his intellectual and social abilities in a number of ways, and our test results were very interesting. We found him to be as intelligent as we thought he'd be. His IQ was in the top 5 percent of the population and his other mental abilities were nearly as high. The personality tests revealed that he was a competitive but caring man who wanted to be socially involved. All of these findings were consistent with his earlier success in sales, but not with his present difficulties in his new job.

A possible answer to Markus's mystery was found when we tested his nonverbal abilities. Markus did very well on almost all kinds of nonverbal skills except for one, paralanguage. When he was asked to identify the emotion carried in the recorded voices of individuals repeating the same simple sentence to represent different emotions, Markus did very poorly. In fact, he scored at a level comparable to a five-year-old child. It was clear that Markus did not have a clue about how people were feeling by listening to their tones of voice. The key to his present problems became clear when we found out that most of his interactions with others now took place on the phone rather than face-to-face. Because of his weakness in picking up how his callers were feeling, Markus was mishandling the very people that he was so good at handling when he could see them and talk to them in person. With this knowledge of a possible reason for his job difficulties, we gave Markus a number of options of how to deal with his problems. These included moving to a different job that would take advantage of his visual nonverbal skills, working on improving his ability to recognize emotion in voices, and redesigning his job so less of it would take place on the phone. We were all optimistic about his future.

Paralanguage is in many ways a unique channel of nonverbal communication. One of its most important features is its ability to remain out of awareness. However, paralanguage is an excellent example of box three information because other people usually are more aware of our voice tones than we are. Think about your own voice for a moment. Remember the times you have heard your own voice on a tape recording. Did you like what you heard? If you are like most of the people to whom we pose this question, you would answer a resounding "No."

When you hear it, you probably grimace and might say to those around you something like, "That doesn't sound like me, does it?" "Yes it does," say your friends, and you have to accept that your voice sounds bad. But then you do something very strange; you simply forget about how bad your voice sounds and do nothing to change it. That is comparable to looking in your mirror before you go out, noticing that you have a piece of celery hanging from your teeth, and deciding to do nothing about it. Very few individuals we talk with have done anything to change their disliked voices and are hard pressed to come up with a good reason why they haven't tried. Some of you might say it is too difficult to change your voice, and, in truth, it is hard to do, but it is far from impossible. You can change the loudness, pitch, intensity, and other aspects of your voice with some practice. What makes change difficult is that paralanguage falls so quickly out of awareness that it is hard to remain aware of and control your newly acquired voice patterns.

Tone of Voice

We use tone of voice to communicate how we are feeling. How we say something can be much more important than what we say. This is consistent with the nonverbal principle of incongruence that we introduced earlier, in the introduction. Here, we use it to mean that when your words disagree with your tone of voice, most people will believe what you are communicating with your tone of voice. *Paralinguistic sarcasm* is a special case of incongruence in communication in which words and tone of voice differ in their emotional meeting. Examples of sarcasm are numerous: "You look great." "Nice throw." "Great looking outfit." "You really did well on the test." All these statements are positive, but when said with a contrasting sarcastic tone of voice they communicate just the opposite meaning. Likewise, all the following are negative statements: "You jerk." "Just who do you think you are." "You're awful." "You shouldn't have done that." However, if they are said with a positive voice, they become extremely positive communications. Inability to understand when someone is being sarcastic with you—or, conversely, is giving you a complement by using negative words with a positive tone of voice—can make you or them feel foolish.

Practicing Incongruent Communication

Sensitivity to the incongruence that might exist between the emotional meanings of voice and words is built on the ability to understand and express words with tones that reflect different feelings. Get an audiotape recorder and practice with the following list of sayings. Say each statement with a tone of voice that is at first consistent with the saying, then follow that by using a tone of voice inconsistent with it.

1. You look wonderful.
2. Great party.
3. Is that your hat?
4. You are so dumb.
5. You are terrible.
6. That is really a nice outfit.
7. What is your business here?
8. Is that what you are going to wear?
9. I hate you.

Tone of voice is one of the earliest and most basic ways of communicating emotion. Human beings use this type of paralinguistic cue to connect with others long before they ever use words. When coupled with rhythm, paralanguage can be a particularly potent source of interpersonal information. Sometimes, though, we may overinterpret these nonverbal messages, as was the case of little baby Richie.

Paralanguage and Rhythm in an Infant—Richie

Jim and Joan absolutely loved their new baby. He was named Richard Newlin after his grandmother and great uncle, but he was called Richie from the moment of his birth. Not surprisingly, Jim and Joan thought he was just about the best-looking and brightest child in the world. They constantly reported his latest achievement so that we could be aware how far ahead of other children he was. One day Joan called Marshall to tell him about Richie's latest accomplishment. According to Joan, Richie, who had just had his six-month birthday, could understand verbal language. Joan excitedly related that when asked "How big is baby Richie?," the infant responded by flinging his arms out as wide as he could. When Marshall was a bit incredulous about Richie's ability to respond to words at his age, Joan said she'd show us the next time they visited. Sure enough, two days later, Jim, Joan, and Richie came to call on Marshall.

After they were settled comfortably in the den, they placed Richie on a pillow in the center of the room and with a look of smug arrogance on his face, Jim moved in front of him. Looking right at Richie, Jim, with a bright big smile on his face and wide-open eyes, said in a sing-song voice, "How big is baby Richie?" As predicted, baby Richie flung his arms out in his now-famous "so big" movement. While baby Richie was a very cute toddler, Marshall had no doubt that he was responding to his father's nonverbal behaviors, and not to his words. With Jim and Joan's permission, Marshall tried an experiment. He got in front of baby Richie and, after he had his attention, said in the same sing-song voice used by Jim, and with a large smile on his face, "Pizza pie and ice cream." As Marshall expected, baby Richie once again flung his arms out in the "so big" movement. Richie, indeed, was responding not to the words, but to the nonverbal tone of voice and rhythm of others.

Animals, like young children, can also mistakenly be believed to understand the spoken word. How many of us have had the experience of saying to our dog, "Want to go for a walk?" and having your pet excitedly respond? While we may think our dog understands our words, it is most likely responding instead to our rhythmic tone of voice, the same way baby Richie did. As we tested baby Richie, test your pet to see if we're right. The next time you are planning to take your dog for a walk, say "Pizza pie and ice cream" with the same rhythm and tone of voice you'd use to say "Let's go for a walk," and see if your pet doesn't react the same.

Emphasis and Variation in Speech

Not only does our tone of voice affect the meaning of the words we use, but so does the way we emphasize and vary our word inflection. Take the sentence "Mary gave me her book." With variation and emphasis, the sentence can have many different meanings depending on which word is emphasized. We'll describe what changing the word emphasis does to the meaning of the sentence.

Mary gave me her book. (Mary is the one who gave me the book, not Bill or Martha.)
Mary *gave* me her book. (Mary didn't sell it to me, she gave it to me.)
Mary gave *me* her book. (She gave the book to me and nobody else.)
Mary gave me *her* book. (Mary gave me the book that belonged to her, and not somebody else's.)
Mary gave me her *book*. (Mary gave me her book and not something else like her shoes or writing tablet.)

Variation in Volume

The richness of meaning in the example about Mary and her book comes about primarily through putting the emphasis on different words. Imagine how difficult it would be to try and understand what other people are trying to tell us if they didn't emphasize particular words. That's why another aspect of paralanguage—variation in volume—is important. Have you ever had to deal with someone who talked to you in a monotone? We bet you found it difficult to gauge the emotional meaning of the words without the help of vocal emphasis and volume. A popular comedy show called *Win Ben Stein's Money* stars comedian Ben Stein, whose comic delivery utilizes both a deadpan face and voice. But it is not funny to have to try and interact in real life with someone whose voice and face show no emotion.

Variation and emphasis in voice are valuable sources of information for us. We appreciate it when others talk with variation and a "lilt." Can you imagine what Martin Luther King's, "I Have a Dream" speech would have been like if it had been delivered in a monotone? We bet it wouldn't have had anywhere near the impact it's had. When you think about it, you can come up with other examples. Pundits say Al Gore lost the election of 2000 to some extent because he couldn't get rid of his monotone. Jimmy Carter's somewhat halting speech lost out to the more fluid presentations of Ronald Reagan in 1980. In almost all aspects of human interaction, speech with fluidity and variation is more enjoyable and attractive.

Researcher Beth Semic has pointed out how important having an attractive voice can be. She describes attractive voices being full and resonant, with pitch that is neither too high nor too low, and varies during conversation. Her basic assumption is that what sounds beautiful is good. A number of studies have been completed to take a look at what kinds of personalities people with attractive voices were thought to have. In one such study, researchers asked individuals to judge over four hundred voices as being attractive or not. They found that the more attractive the voices were rated, the more positive were the personality characteristics that were assumed (such as warm, industrious, and sensitive).

The implications of paralanguage for business are enormous. The first interaction outsiders may have with a business is through phone contact. Research has even found that a recorded answering machine message can have a real and important impact on the listener. A study gauging the effects of vocal attractiveness and vocal content in answering machine messages found that, regardless of the textual content of the message, those that employed attractive voices were seen as more trustworthy, competent, likeable, and dominant. The old adage is probably correct: It's not what you say, but how you say it.

The Power of Silence—Jimmy and Joyce

One of the unique and overlooked qualities of paralanguage is silence. Silence can have great communicative value, and needless to say, it's use and effects are classic box four material. Most people focus only on what is said, not what goes on between words.

Jimmy was called to Joyce's office to explain why he'd missed the meetings she had called regarding office procedures. He knocked on the door and Joyce called, "Come in." Jimmy opened the door and walked in to the office.

"Sit down," said Joyce. "I was wondering why you didn't show up at yesterday's meeting." Jimmy gave what he thought was a good excuse for his absence, but after he finished, Joyce said nothing. At first Jimmy just sat there and waited for Joyce to say something. As the silence lengthened, however, Jimmy began to squirm about in his chair. "Well," he said, "It's the truth." Joyce still said nothing. Jimmy squirmed some more and beads of sweat began to form on his forehead. "Come on, Joyce, say something."

Joyce spoke then, saying, "I don't believe you."

"I'm not lying," said Jimmy. "Honest." Joyce's response was more silence. Finally, Jimmy shouted, "Okay, Okay, Okay! I lied. I just forgot. I was over at the pub having lunch and I forgot. Are you satisfied?"

"Yes," said Joyce. "Consider yourself written up."

Joyce knew how useful silence can be when communicating. Indeed, silence really can be golden—or it can be hell, depending on how it's used. For Joyce, it was golden; for Jimmy, it was hell.

As with all other types of nonverbal communication, there can be receptive and expressive deficits in the use of silence. People with receptive problems misread messages of silence sent by others. They don't know how to interpret the pauses in speech and may actually talk when they should be quiet. Because of this problem they can appear rude and unfeeling. People who cannot use silence expressively, on the other hand, pause in ways that interrupt and disrupt the flow of conversation. Deborah Tannen, who has studied the conversational styles of men and women, suggests that people who can't tolerate long pauses may often wonder why others don't want to interact, while people who desire long pauses may think others are too talkative and self-centered. It is all too easy to start ascribing unpleasant personality characteristics to others who make us feel uncomfortable. The process becomes all the more potentially harmful if it takes place out of awareness (in box four).

In terms of our relationship model (see chapter 1), too much silence at the beginning of a relationship is inappropriate. Instead, small talk is what is needed to get the relationship off and running. However, if the relationship is going to deepen, then a person needs the skill and knowledge to know how to use silence judiciously. Then silence will truly be golden for everyone involved.

Paralanguage is unique among the nonverbal channels of communication in that it occurs along with and between the words that make up our verbal language. In this sense, it can have the most direct effect on the impact of what we say verbally. However, all of the channels of nonverbal language have the power to modify verbal messages to others. Interestingly, the process does not work the same in reverse—no matter what we say verbally, it is very difficult to change the effects that our tone of voice or facial expressions have on others. Though less central, the other forms of nonverbal language are equally as capable of affecting our relationships for good or ill. To be sure, we want you to focus on your paralanguage and facial expressions as you try to bring as much nonverbal awareness as possible into box one; however, to ignore the power of touch, postures, gestures, and style of dress would be most unwise.

Chapter 5

Channels of Nonverbal Behavior: Touch, Postures, Gestures, and Fashion

So that you are fully informed about the places in boxes two, three, and four that you will need to look to determine if you are dyssemic, we will now describe the final forms of nonverbal communication: touch, postures, gestures, and fashion. These channels of nonverbal behavior are at once more concrete and more peripheral to your ongoing social interactions than those we've previously described. But don't be fooled into thinking that they are unimportant because we are presenting them last. Every aspect of nonverbal communication makes a unique contribution to relationship outcomes, and each has to be mastered if you want to be interpersonally successful.

Touch

Expressive Dyssemia for Touch—Ginny

Ginny was a toucher. Whenever anyone came within an arm's reach of her, they got touched. Whomever she faced in conversation would be touched on his or her arms or hands. The truth is that Ginny wasn't real sure of herself and always seemed tense. When anyone talked with her it wasn't long before she'd give a nervous little laugh and then touch the person. Most everyone "sort of" liked Ginny, but almost to a person they also wished she wouldn't touch them so frequently. At parties she would come up behind people and touch them on the back. Just before she touched people she'd always give a tittering, annoying laugh first. People didn't mind being touched by her at first, but it soon got to be a habit that made them uncomfortable. What made it all the more difficult was that Ginny just didn't seem to have a clue that her touching annoyed others. Because of the rules that surround nonverbal communication, even those that were aware of the source of their discomfort with her were hesitant to tell her. Instead, they just spent less and less time with her. One result of being rejected in this manner was that Ginny didn't know it was her touching behavior that was driving them away. Her being abandoned in this manner led to her feeling more and more on edge, and that actually increased her frequency of touching people.

Why should Ginny's touching be such a bother? Part of the answer is that because we touch so little in our culture, its overuse or misuse has unique negative impacts on us. We usually don't like to be touched by others, especially if we haven't given them our permission. Yet the use of touch, especially in our close relationships, is an extremely powerful way of communicating intimate feelings. It is ironic that a major reason we aren't very adept at using touch is because we don't use it very much. Desmond Morris, perhaps the best-known investigator of nonverbal behavior, has put it this way: "We often talk about the way we talk, and we frequently try to see the way we see, but for some reason we rarely touch on the way we touch."

We know that touch is important to us early in our lives. Not receiving enough human contact when we are babies can have profoundly negative effects on our psychological, physical, and emotional adjustment. In their important book on touching behavior, Ronald B. Adler and Neil Towne suggest that touching is essential to our healthy development. They report that during the nineteenth and early twentieth centuries, a large percentage of children born every year died from a disease called *marasmus*, which translated from the Greek means "wasting away." In some orphanages the mortality rate was nearly 100 percent, but even children from the most progressive homes, hospitals, and other institutions where their physical needs were met also died from the ailment. Adler and Towne conclude that just meeting infants' biological needs was not enough to sustain them. What the infants were missing, and what they needed in order to grow and thrive, was the touch and contact of others.

What was true for these infants is also true for us as adults. We need something more than simply having our basic biological needs met. We need to touch and be touched in order to be assured that we are valued and cared for. Some of you may even be suffering now from the negative effects of touch deprivation during your early years and may unknowingly use unhealthy methods such as drinking alcohol or taking other drugs to deaden the pain of feeling alone and disconnected.

Touch and Age

How much people are likely to be touched changes considerably with age. Children, especially girls, receive increasing amounts of touch beginning in infancy and peaking at about four years of age. From kindergarten through sixth grade, however, there is a decline in the amount of touching children experience, and the decline sharpens during the middle-school years. In fact, it appears that children experience touch about half as often in middle school as they do in primary school. The frequency of being touched continues to decline throughout the rest of the life span, with the elderly receiving the least contact of all. While the decrease in touch we experience as we age could be explained by peoples' fear of their touch being misinterpreted as a sexual message, this does not account for why older people are touched the least of all. It is ironic that older adults, who probably need touch and contact more than any other age group, receive it the least.

Rules for Using Touch

Regardless of when touch is experienced, it is fair to say that its use is a "touchy" subject. Touch probably has more residual rules governing its function than any of the other nonverbal behaviors. Perhaps this is true, in part, because if people are close enough to touch us, they also are potentially close enough to physically hurt us. Touch often can be construed by us as negative, and yet it is the true coin of the realm when it comes to communicating closeness and caring. And what sort of help and guidance do we get from our elders regarding what to do with this most powerful nonverbal behavior? Not much, except for admonitions such as "Don't touch!" or "Keep your hands to yourself!" But if we don't touch, how are we supposed to learn the appropriate use of patting, slapping, stroking, shaking, holding, guiding, tickling, poking, pinching, embracing, and grooming, to name just a few of the thousands of different types of touch? And what about hugging, that wonderful touching behavior that allows us to express closeness to those we hold dear. How many of the dozens of different hugs that have been identified do you know how to use?

One of your authors believed hugging to be such an important skill that when he noticed one of his children hugging others like they were so many inanimate objects, he spent weeks teaching the child to hug correctly. We won't say which of the authors or which of the children were involved, but we will tell you that *all* of our children have grown up to be first-class huggers!

We wonder, though, what kind of teaching experiences you've had in using hugging or any of the other kinds of touching behaviors that are so important in signaling movement from the acquaintance phase of a relationship to something deeper and more meaningful? Without this kind of social knowledge, you may misuse touch and hamper your ongoing relationships.

Increasing Your Awareness of Touch

Stanley Jones, one of the most prolific researchers of touch behavior, has suggested some exercises for helping people to understand it better. We think they will help you to become more aware of the frequency and meaning of your own and others' touch behavior.

1. Keep a record of your own touches for one or more complete days using the Touch Recording Form (see Appendix B). Record every contact and indicate if it was initiated by you or someone else, was mutually initiated (like a hug or a handshake), or whether the initiator was unclear (accidental touches). When you are done, count up the touches.
2. Were you more of a toucher or a touchee? How many touches did you experience per day? (Average for females is twelve; average for males is eight.)

    A. With whom did you have most touches? (What kind of relationship do you have with them?)
    B. What meanings did *you* communicate? Were there some rejected touches? If so, why? Are there other meanings you would like to communicate? Observe and record the touches of others in some popular environmental location—airports, railway stations, and bus terminals are good places for obser-

vation, especially at departures. Another appropriate place for observing parents and children is preschools at the beginning or end of the day. Use the same categories as in number 1. Count up the touches.

i. What differences in touching did you observe for men with men, women with women, and men with women? (You could also look at the differences between mothers and fathers with sons and daughters.)
ii. Did you notice any other nonverbal behaviors that preceded good-byes (or hellos), like waving, extending arms for a touch, and so forth?

3. What changes would you like to make in your touch behavior? Try out one of those changes and see what happens.

Expressive Touch Dyssemia—Trey

After the service, people were standing around in the hall, talking and having coffee. Trey had gotten his cup of coffee and spotted James and Eloise over in the corner. He really wanted to ask James about the possibility of being chosen to be on the planning committee to search for a new minister. Trey had strong feelings about the characteristics any new pastor should possess, and wanted to be sure James understood that. As he hurried his way through the crowd, Trey bumped into a number of people, forcing some of them to spill their drinks. A trail of damp suits, dresses, and flooring marked his path. James was standing with his back to Trey. When Trey was close enough, he reached out and clasped James's left shoulder with a vise-like grip to get his attention. James quickly turned, around spilling his coffee in all directions and exclaimed in a loud voice, "What the—!" Trey was startled himself at James's reaction and, in turn, his coffee went flying in all directions, with most of it falling on Eloise.

• • •

Trey is an *expressive touch dyssemic.* He is not aware of what his touch communicates to others. He showed his lack of awareness of the boundaries of others by bumping into them as he walked through the after-church crowd, and if bumping into them wasn't bad enough, he also failed to say "excuse me" or "sorry." Trey was unaware of how upset he was making everyone he jostled. Not only was he invading others' personal space by banging into them, but he was also bursting through their personal-space bubble, touching them at zero interpersonal distance. Although Trey had already broken a number of rules about touch on his bumpy way to James, their negative impact paled when compared to what resulted from his attempt to get James's attention from behind.

In most social situations, there is a preferred way to get people's attention when we approach them from behind, and believe us, it is not to silently sneak up on them and suddenly grab their shoulder with all your strength. The correct method, which most of us understand, is to take one finger—usually the index finger on your right hand—and tap them ever-so-lightly on about a one-inch-square spot on their shoulder, usually the left one, equidistant from the neck and the end of the shoulder. This touching behavior is always accompanied by a soft "excuse me," or its equivalent.

Think about all that we are required to know and do in order to simply touch others appropriately from behind. First, we must know *where to touch.* Only that one small area of the shoulder is appropriate; anywhere else of the back of the person is inappropriate in this situation. We cannot touch in the middle of the back, or along side the shoulder, or behind the knee, or along the waist, or anywhere else except for that one-inch-square place on the shoulder.

Next, we must know that *the touch has to be light.* Any other kind of touch is improper. We cannot poke, pound, prod, pinch, or otherwise contact the one-inch square area with any intensity. We must also know that the touch *has to be made with only one finger.* Any other appendage or number of appendages would be inappropriate. We cannot use three fingers, a fist, an open hand, two hands, or an elbow or a foot. The only acceptable choice in this situation is your one finger, usually your index finger.

Finally, we must know that the light, one-fingered touch *is accompanied by some soft vocalization* that communicates we are apologizing because we have traveled through the largest part of a person's personal-space bubble to arrive at an intimate distance, and he or she has yet to see us or be aware that we are there. We have broken some very important residual rules about personal-space usage by approaching the person in this manner, and we want him or her to know we mean no harm. If, as we approach, we never get any closer than about four feet, and if we move around to be in front of the person, none of the above behaviors is necessary. But if what we have to say is so important, or something prevents us from approaching so that the person can see us, then we must follow the rules outlined above or suffer the interpersonal consequences.

We need to be aware that almost every act of touching is as complex as the shoulder touch, and requires social knowledge and skill to complete successfully. Appropriate touching behavior is learned and varies considerably from one culture to another. In our culture, strict rules exist about where on the body it is proper to touch someone. If we are going to touch people, it is acceptable, for example, to touch them briefly along the outside of their body-line, on the outside of the arms and legs. However, we must be aware that moving our touch just a few inches to the inside parts of the arms and legs changes the emotional message completely from one of getting attention to one of emotional and physical intimacy. It is one thing to pat people lightly and briefly on the outside of their arms to communicate that they have done a job well; it is quite another if that touch is a long, lingering one on the inside areas of their arms or legs. Not only the *location*, but the *duration* of a touch is loaded with emotional meaning of which we must be aware to be socially successful. Remember, of all the nonverbal channels, touch is the one in which errors in usage are tolerated least.

Categories of Touching

Investigators like psychologist Richard Heslin have attempted to categorize touch by the type of message that is being sent, in order to make it potentially easier to understand and study. We think Heslin's system is a good one because not only is it scientifically sound but because it also makes good common sense. Heslin uses relationship terms to classify touching on a continuum of intimacy. You should be able to categorize your own and others' touching behavior according to this system. You also might try to apply it to the touching exercises presented earlier, in "Increasing Your Awareness of Touch."

Functional-Professional

This kind of touch is often referred to as *cold touch* because people are being touched to accomplish some goal or task or to provide a service that could not be accomplished otherwise. Examples of cold touch include having a suit tailored, undergoing physical therapy, or having a medical examination. Even though we may be touched in some unusual ways and in some surprising places during these interactions, touch does not convey an intimate or sexual message.

Just because touch is classified as cold doesn't mean it still can't affect our behavior. For example, psychologists A. Crusco and

C. Wetzel completed a fascinating study on the tipping behavior of customers, entitled "The Midas Touch." In their study, they had waitresses do one of three things when they returned with the credit slip or change after settling the customer's bill. In the first instance, the waitress fleetingly touched the diner's palm with her fingers for one-half second. In the second instance, the waitress placed her hand on the diner's shoulder for one second. In the third, the waitress had no physical contact with the customer. The analysis of the customers' tipping behavior showed that both the shoulder touch and the fleeting hand touch increased the amount of tipping over no touch at all. The effect of touch on tipping behavior did not differ between men and women customers.

Social-Polite

Heslin says that the purpose of touch in this category is to "affirm the other person's identity as a member of the same species, operating by essentially the same rules of conduct." Probably the best example of a nonverbal touch behavior in this category is the handshake. Because the handshake is the only generally acceptable way for most people to initiate contact with one another in our culture, much information is transferred through this act.

Roger Axtell has studied the do's and don'ts of body language across the world. In his useful and very funny book, *Gestures: The Do's and Taboos of Body Language around the World,* Axtell reports that the handshaking advice of his father—"to look them straight in the eye and give 'em a good firm grasp"—is not followed universally. Males from the Middle East, for example, are instructed to give a gentle grip, because a firm grip is considered to be too aggressive. The French, according to Axtell, are the most handshakingest of all, shaking hands when greeting, departing, and returning. In fact, Peter Mayle, in his wonderfully entertaining book *A Year in Provence,* described

Frenchmen as wanting to shake hands so much that when their hands were full or dirty they would give their pinky finger to be shook. Most Americans would be satisfied with a good head-nod and probably wouldn't quite know what to make of another man offering his pinky finger.

Friendship-Warmth

Touch that communicates friendship and caring is a very important behavior. As we pointed out in chapter 2, even though verbal language may stay the same, one of the major indicators of a relationship's deepening takes place nonverbally through changes in the way we touch and use personal space. According to Heslin, (and we agree), this kind of touch sends the message that the person being touched is unique and not just like everyone else. For example, a handshake used to indicate acquaintanceship may be expanded to communicate friendship by grasping the arm of the other person at the bicep or by placing the free hand over the top of the hand that is being shook. Morley Safer, the longtime reporter for CBS, once said that President Clinton was adept at using subtle changes in handshakes to communicate warmth and friendship to those he met.

Love-Intimacy

Touch is perhaps the most important way we communicate love for another. By laying our hand on the cheek of other people or by fully embracing them, we are saying strongly that we love them. Because the full embrace is one of the most commonly used touch behaviors to communicate love and caring, maybe we should spend a moment or two on it.

The full embrace should be familiar to you: It is when two

people are pressed close together frontally, with the sides of their heads in contact and their arms wrapped around one another's bodies. One of the interesting sex differences here is that while the full embrace can take place with same- or opposite-sex pairings, men are more prone to use the side-to-side hug, in which one arm is wrapped around the other but their heads are apart. Next time you get a chance to watch heterosexual men embrace one another, watch them closely and chances are you will see an interesting sequence of action. During the embrace the men will pat each other rhythmically on the back about three times with their hands and then quickly break from the embrace. It is as though the men are assuring themselves by the timed and rhythmic patting that the embrace is time-limited and has no sexual implications.

Before we leave this category, we want you to know that touch used to convey love-intimacy varies considerably from person to person and from couple to couple. Those who love one another can be very creative in coming up with kinds and patterns of touch to communicate their caring for one another.

According to Desmond Morris, all intimate touch, if used appropriately, serves to soothe and comfort us. Morris describes how we usually go about getting our much-needed doses of intimate touch.

- When we are feeling nervous or depressed, a loved one may attempt to reassure us by giving us a comforting hug or a squeeze of the hand.
- In the absence of a loved one, it may have to be one of the specialist touchers, such as a doctor, who pats our arm and tells us not to worry.
- If our only company is our pet dog or cat, we may take it in our arms and press our cheek to its furry body to feel the comfort of its warm touch.
- If we are completely alone and some sinister noise startles

us in the night, we may hug the bedclothes tightly around us to feel secure in their soft embrace.

- If all else fails, we still have our own bodies, and we can hug, embrace, clasp, and touch ourselves in a great variety of ways to help soothe away our fears.

Gestures

There can be little doubt that touching is a very powerful form of communication. The use of the hands to communicate is not limited to touch, however, because in addition to touching other people physically we can also signal an incredible number of things to them merely through the position or movement of our hands. Extend the positions and movements to our arms and we are capable of literally tens of thousands of gestures that play an integral part in our everyday interactions and relationships.

One important difference between gestures and touching is that we do not need to be close to people to communicate with them through gestures. Along with postures and fashion—which we'll describe later in this chapter—we classify gestures as long-distance signals. These are most important in the choice and beginnings of relationships, because, before we decide to strike up a conversation or approach other people, we typically try to learn all we can about them from these long-distance nonverbal signs. We look at how they hold their hands and arms. We look at their postures—how they stand, how they walk. Finally, we look at how they are dressed. All this takes place before we get to what most people think are the more important nonverbal cues: the look on their faces, the sound of their voices, and what they are actually saying (which *are* more important for later stages of relationships). Make no mistake, however, unless our long-distance communicators are effective, we don't need to worry about how we look or sound or what we say, because few people will get close enough to us for a long enough time for us to prove that their long-distance impressions were off the mark.

The person who has problems in the areas of gestures, postures, and fashion is often described something like this: "He's a great guy once you get to know him!" What this may mean is that the long-distance signs suggest something different from what the up-close and personal signs tell. This is a classic example of an expressive dyssemia where what is being communicated is not an accurate reflection of what a person truly is feeling or meaning to communicate. This was Kevin's problem.

Expressive Dyssemia for Gestures—Kevin

Kevin was a thirty-six-year-old high school math teacher. His students thought he was terrific, while the parents of the students found him cold and unlikable. The discrepancy between the students' and their parents' perceptions, it turned out, was based on the fact that the students spent enough time with Kevin to get past his off-putting initial impression, but their parents did not. Kevin rarely moved his hands or arms. He did not use his hands to emphasize his words. Kevin's gestures didn't change when he discussed topics that he was excited about, versus those he was less interested in.

Kevin came to our attention because he received poor teaching ratings based on limited observations made by his principal and out-of-school evaluators from the county school system. To them, Kevin was a poor teacher, but in reality his students liked and respected him, learned math, and always gave him high ratings despite the fact that he was a tough grader. Kevin had an expressive gestural/postural dyssemia. Fortunately, as you will see in chapters 7 and 8, correcting this kind of dyssemia can be relatively easy when you can read gestures and postures well in others. A few hours of self-observation in his classroom, with a chance to read his own gestural and postural information, resulted in some significant shifts in Kevin's long-distance *short-term* impact.

Making Yourself Aware of Gestures

As we encouraged Kevin to do with videotapes of his teaching, try to focus your attention on the gestures going on around you every day. Here's a good exercise to help you do that.

On a given day, decide that you are going to look at people's hands whenever you can. We don't suggest that you stare at their hands when you should be looking at their eyes or faces; however, when you are in a group meeting, for example, and other people are addressing the speaker or you are part of an audience attending to a speaker, break your gaze away from the face of the person talking and look at the hands of those around you. You will be amazed at how much "leakage" there is in our hand movements. People who are sitting attentively and looking dutifully at a speaker can often be seen twiddling their thumbs or showing other clear signs of impatience or boredom.

Look at your hands. What are you saying to others inadvertently? Look at the hands of people who are sitting at nearby tables in restaurants. Next time you are in a museum, try this exercise: Hold your index finger horizontally across your visual field and block the faces of the characters in a painting. Now look at their hands. Even though you were not initially aware of the hand positions and gestures, you can now see them more vividly. However, we can assure you that even when you were not consciously aware of them, your brain was registering them.

Gestures are probably more culturally determined and variable than most of the other nonverbal parts of speech. That is, a gesture that means one thing in the United States, or even in one city in the United States, can mean quite another elsewhere. Anthropologist Desmond Morris, whom we quoted earlier in our discussion of touch, was among the first to present scientific research on how gestures differed in their meaning from one country to another. Roger Axtell, whom we mentioned a few pages back, has also provided "translation" dictionaries for people living and working in different cultures, to prevent them from making gestural mistakes. For instance, one of the most common American hand gestures—the "okay" sign made by touching the tip of our index finger to the tip of our thumb to form a circle and by flaring out the other three fingers in a fanlike position—is not okay in many other countries. In France, for example, the same signal is taken to mean that something is worthless; in Japan, it signifies money; and in some South American and Mediterranean countries, it is an insult referring to the female genitalia—talk about a potential business or social faux pas!

Axtell learned early that we must speak two languages—verbal and nonverbal—if we are to function fully and effectively in society. While his book is chock-full of really interesting and evocative examples of ways to communicate gesturally in places all over the world, what he says of business relationships is equally true of social relationships. We must be aware of what we are communicating with our gestures *and* what others may be communicating to us. When we can read other people's gestures effectively, we increase our chances of succeeding both socially and vocationally. When we cannot, we may be receptively dyssemic for gestures, as was Brandy, the young woman we describe next.

Receptive Dyssemia for Gestures—Brandy

Brandy was a nineteen-year-old college student whose friends described her as "ditzy." While most of the time they used this label as a term of endearment, Brandy found that few serious potential men were drawn to her "ditziness." Brandy sought help at her college counseling center because, as she put it, "I have plenty of guy friends, but no one really seemed interested in me in a long term kind of way." The first thing that her interviewer noticed as he introduced himself to her was that Brandy looked downward when she spoke and walked. The interview was uncomfortable for both participants. Though she tried to answer questions to the best of her ability, Brandy often spoke longer than was appropriate because she did not notice the interviewer's many nonverbal cues to stop. Likewise, she didn't pick up the cues for her to begin talking when the interviewer stopped. Brandy seemed unable to pick up when it was her turn to talk in the conversation. What was happening was that she was not picking up the gestural and postural cues of the interviewer, the cues that we all use to communicate, "I'm finished talking, now it's your turn." Among these cues are a cessation of hand gestures associated with our talking, a turn of our head in the direction of the listener, a shifting of our eyes directly to the other person, changes in our voice inflection, and the like.

To be sure, there are more than gestures in the give-and-take of interpersonal communication. As he began to sum up the meeting with Brandy, the interviewer sat forward on his chair, straightened his back, and put his hands on his knees—all signs that say, "this is about to come to an end." Upon seeing these cues, most people mirror the same position to a large extent, begin to gather up their things and, for sure, do not start a new conversation topic. Brandy remained seated back in her chair, did not reach for her books and backpack, and said, "I think my brother had troubles like I do. There was this one time that he was in high school . . ." She proceeded to tell a five-minute story that might have been relevant twenty minutes earlier, but not at this closing stage of the interview. It was clear that Brandy was not picking up gestural cues and as a result probably made people pretty uncomfortable when it came to carrying on and ending conversations.

In a lighter vein, some of you may be familiar with a wonderful short essay by Woody Allen, "A Little Louder, Please," in which he described a character who in essence was a receptive dyssemic for gestures. In the following excerpt, Woody's character has been invited to a theater performance that turns out to be a mime who is silently presenting a play called *Going on a Picnic.* He describes his character's impressions of what the mime was trying to communicate as follows.

> It all began when a wisp of a man walked onstage in kitchen-white makeup and a tight black leotard. Standard picnic dress. . . . The mime now proceeded to spread a picnic blanket, and, instantly, my old confusion set in. He was either spreading a picnic blanket or milking a small goat. Next, he elaborately removed his shoes, except that I'm not positive they were his shoes, because he drank one of them and mailed the other to Pittsburgh. I say "Pittsburgh," but actually it is hard to mime the concept of Pittsburgh, and as I look back on it, I now think what he was miming was not Pittsburgh at all but a man driving a golf cart through a revolving door—or possibly two men dismantling a printing press.

Through his unique humor, Woody Allen shows how difficult it can be for someone with gestural dyssemia to understand the world. The same is true for anyone who has trouble using the next channel of nonverbal communication, postures.

Postures

We have been looking at various nonverbal "parts of speech" as we would through a camera while backing away from our subject. We started with close-ups of eyes and faces and then drew back to incorporate hand positions and hand and arm gestures. Now, let's pull back still another step and consider some full-length snapshots of people, pictures that include their entire bodies, pictures that allow us to see and read the meaning of postures.

Postures are very powerful long-distance communicators. We use posture and its dynamic equivalent, style of walking, to size up people who are approaching us on a street. We try to read people's postures at parties or other social gatherings and use what we read to decide whether or not to approach them and strike up a conversation. Indeed, long before people have seen our own faces or heard our voices, they have an impression of us from the way we stand and move.

Some years ago, we were teaching in England and attended a local theater production in Canterbury. One of the characters in the play was an American, who was in this instance portrayed by a British actor. He appeared on stage in a large white hat and jeans and stood with his back straight, chest out, and hands arrogantly resting on his hips (the so-called "arms akimbo" position). This was not meant to be a caricature, we later learned, but was simply what was believed to be an accurate depiction of American posture! We wanted to disagree, but just as we began to speak we noticed that, in our frustration, we had assumed this John Wayne posture ourselves!

Postures are not only important for actors communicating information in theater, but also for businesspeople, educators, physicians, lawyers—in fact, for most all of us in our everyday interactions. We have a physician friend who tells us that he gets a good idea of how sick his patients are simply by glancing at their sitting posture in the waiting room before he officially greets them. Some teachers we know can judge the kind of day they are about to have by looking at how their students are sitting or standing before class begins. Many a salesperson is successful because he or she can read the difference between the stance of someone who is seriously interested in buying versus someone who is just looking. In truth, the ways people stand, sit, and walk provide surprising amounts of useful interpersonal information.

Next time you are in an office or waiting room, watch the postures of people there. Do their postures seem to fit with their level of employment? Is the lower-level employee slouching and looking unmotivated? Is the higher-level person walking with an aura of determination and a spring in his or her step? It's hard to know which of these comes first, but we do know that effective posture communication and success tend to go together.

Expressive Dyssemia for Postures—Ameesh

We once worked with a college junior, Ameesh, who was extremely bright; however, Ameesh walked all hunched over. When he sat, he slouched. When he listened to people in lectures or in conversations, he held his head up with the palm of his hand, with his fingers curled against his cheek. His posture and gait said that he was totally bored with everyone and everything. When we mentioned his head resting on his hand, he said that he always felt tired and that he really was not bored. However, we reminded him that other people, especially teachers and prospective employers, do not and ought not have to keep up with our own personal sleep habits. If other people see us leaning our heads against our hands, they assume we are bored and they act on that assumption. We videotaped Ameesh so he could see how he came across posturally. He seemed surprised by what he saw. This insight into how he appeared motivated him to work on changing his resting posture. *Resting posture* functions much like the resting face that we told you about earlier. It's the posture we assume when we are not particularly feeling anything—our neutral position. We asked Ameesh to think about his resting posture and what it was saying to other people. The result was a change in his resting posture and positive changes in his initial attempts to begin relationships.

• • •

As a long-distance communicator, our resting posture is one of the main cues others use in deciding whether to invite us into beginning a relationship. Our research and observations have shown us that people whose resting postures are positive, upright, and "ready to go" tend to be liked more by others. Imagine walking into a workroom filled with strangers. Imagine further that all the tables have at least one person at them, so you will need to share. At one table is someone with a positive resting face and resting posture. At another is someone with a moderate scowl on his face, slouched in his chair and hunched over the table. With whom would you usually choose to sit?

Let's say that your answer to this question is either "I don't know, they're both the same to me" or "I think the slouching guy would be fun to meet." If this is the case, you might be like Betsy, a very nice woman we met who turned out to be receptively dyssemic for postures.

Receptive Dyssemia for Postures—Betsy

Betsy came to us with relationship problems, specifically in choosing people with whom to relate. She described herself as someone who always seemed to pick out people who turned out to be bad for her. By this she meant that she wanted to be with people who liked to have quiet conversations, go to movies, read books, and go to classical music concerts. Typically, however, she would find herself having first, but rarely second, dates with men who wanted to party. We formally assessed Betsy's nonverbal processing skills and found that she had trouble identifying internal emotional states that typically go with various postures. She liked the guys whose postures suggested just what she *didn't* want—the party guys!

• • •

As with most dyssemias, Betsy's was correctable with awareness and practice. She also needed to stop trying to meet men at general social events and to look for them at more appropriate sites, such as bookstores, classical music events, and clubs. Our assessment revealed that Betsy also had trouble with expressive postural language: She tended to walk, stand, and sit more like a "party" person than the quieter, intellectual woman she felt herself to be. In this regard, she was actually sending out cues to attract the very sort of men who she ultimately found to be wrong for her. In large measure, she attracted them not primarily through her posture, however, but rather through her style of dress and use of fashion, the next and final nonverbal part of speech we will consider in this chapter.

Fashion

Fashion includes anything with communication value that might be attached to, put on, or done to our bodies. Thus, clothing, jewelry, perfumes or colognes, and the length and style (or even absence of) our hair are all examples of fashion, or what some researchers call *objectics.* Few would disagree that how we dress and groom ourselves is critically important in determining our impact on others, and even on ourselves when we glance in a mirror. People spend a good deal of time dealing with this avenue of nonverbal communication, both in choosing the things they will use to decorate their bodies and in being sure that they fit or are applied "just right." Indeed, fashion can be a most potent form of long- and short-distance communication.

The link between how we dress and our degree of success has been known for some time. In his classic book called *Dress for Success,* John T. Molloy told millions of businesspeople about the possible effects that attire can have on the process and eventual outcome of their business ventures. More recently, Sherry

Maysonave has brought Molloy's notions into the new millennium with her book *Casual Power,* in which she explains to people how to dress *down* rather than *up* for success. Times and styles change, to be sure, but what does not change is the fact that how we dress affects how well we do socially and vocationally. People who know how to use the expressive and receptive languages of clothing, accessories, hairstyle, and other fashion cues are clearly a step up on others in establishing and maintaining solid productive relationships. But as with all the nonverbal channels of communication, there are some people whose interpersonal and work-related experiences are far from optimal because of the way they use fashion cues.

Fashion Dyssemia—Noah

Noah is a twenty-five-year-old office worker at a large newspaper. His work has him interacting with people all day long. Others have come to value his skills and he is seen as a satisfactory worker. He is dependable and well mannered and enjoys being around others. Sadly, he is not as successful once he leaves the office and attempts to generate a social life. Noah is one of those people who tries too hard to look good and is not aware of how widely he is missing the fashion mark. To begin with, Noah uses an enormous amount of aftershave lotion. To his way of thinking, if a little of something smells good, then more of it will smell even better. As a result, while Noah assumes he is beginning his interactions with others with a pleasing scent, in actuality he is driving most prospective relationship partners away before things can even get started. Even before his abundant aftershave scent begins to work its negative magic on others, Noah's style of dress warns people that he may not be the best person with whom to begin a relationship. It's not that he dresses poorly or extremely, it's just that he is out of synch with what currently is in style. Inevitably,

Noah will be wearing the prior year's style of clothes, and if he happens to be lucky enough to hit the current year's style correctly, he'll choose seriously mismatched color schemes. What makes this so sad is that Noah thinks he is the height of fashion sense and style, and is unaware that he is jinxing his chances at relationship success by his own efforts.

Fashion cues are a special case among the parts of speech of nonverbal language, representing the most rapidly changing set of nonverbal signs that exist. Whereas a smile has meant happiness since time immemorial, a ring through one's tongue has only recently been seen as a positive cue by some people. Similarly, while a wave of the hand has meant "hello" or "good-bye" for centuries, the communication value of purple hair is of somewhat more recent vintage. Because fashions change so frequently, you must be able to keep up with the cues that constitute appropriate communication. When you don't, the results can be heartbreaking. In modern day culture, to think we are communicating that we are cool and in style when we are not can wreck our lives, especially when we are younger.

Not only do we have to be aware of fashion changes that can take place within a culture over time, but we must also remember the wide differences that exist between cultures. Smiles mean happiness and tears mean sadness in most countries and cultures, but the clothing that is "right" or communicates what we want it to communicate can vary considerably from place to place. For example, at a business meeting in, say, Bahrain, one can be sure that everyone will want to be dressed in what they consider to be proper business attire. However, an American businessperson will wear a standard business suit, while the local businessmen might be wearing traditional robes and headdresses. In New York City, one only has to go to the United Nations to see the broad range of fashion cues people use to show proper respect for and awareness of serious international meetings. We can only imagine how one would go about identifying someone with fashion dyssemia within a culture other than his or her own. It seems that outside of one's own culture, most people will appear to have expressive fashion dyssemia.

Though a difficult topic, we cannot leave our discussion of objectives without a short note about odor. Smelling bad has more of an impact on interactions than smelling good. Body odor, bad breath, the smell of alcohol or dirty clothing, or any other aversive olfactory stimulus can destroy an interaction before it ever has a chance of beginning. Nevertheless, if we have an offensive odor, others will be loath to tell us—instead, they will simply stay away from us. This is the sort of information that is very firmly ensconced in Johari's box three, and few people will ever divulge it unless there is a strong reason. It seems safe to say that, at least in the United States, people need to smell neutrally or somewhat pleasantly if they are going to get past the early stages of any sort of relationship.

You now have the basics for determining if you are dyssemic, where your difficulties may lie, and how they can be interfering with your relationships. It is time now for us to help you get down to the business of being more specific about assessing your nonverbal weaknesses and seeing where in your relationship process you need to improve. We think you are ready for step two. Read on.

Chapter 6

Working with Your Coach

Now that we've had you travel through rhythm, time, and space, focused your attention on your face and voice, and made you aware that even how you stand, move your hands, or put items on your body have important communication meanings, you are ready to continue with your journey toward becoming a more effective user of nonverbal language—to becoming more eusemic. We'd like you to imagine that you are walking along the same path as Kyle, the dyssemic engineer about whom we have spoken several times. Having read the last three chapters, you and Kyle are ready to start looking in places that perhaps you previously did not know even existed—in box four of the Johari Window. It's time to move seriously into step two: identifying the problem, or what is more traditionally and formally termed *assessment*. This will be a challenging yet ultimately rewarding task, and it is one that we think is easier to complete if you can find someone to help you. We call this person a *coach*.

Establishing a Coaching Partnership

A basic truth is that no one will tell you about your own interpersonal strengths and weaknesses unless you give them permission to do so. All of us have been brought up to be polite and not to say something that might hurt another's feelings. This makes box-three tasks all the more difficult. We believe that the best help comes through other people. That means that you must find someone with whom you can have a special relationship, one that is not necessarily deep and intense, but one that can allow you to receive box-three information. This person, your coach, functions as a human mirror, someone in whom your reflection will be more complete than the one you are used to seeing.

When we work with children, it is relatively easier to assess what might be wrong in their nonverbal patterns than it is for adults. For one thing, children are usually in school, and there is a teacher there to observe them for six or seven hours a day over a nine-month period. In addition, children's parents are often able to identify additional problems in social interactional skills. In fact, we have written two books dealing with nonverbal language problems in children that describe the ways that dyssemia can be identified (assessed) and corrected. Working with adults can present some different challenges, and so we have developed a set of procedures that are more appropriate for them. These procedures include ways both to identify problems (move them into box three) and to correct them (move them into box one) so that the possibility of successful relationships is increased. While helpful observers are the key for aiding children and adults who don't fit in, the specific people involved differ. For children, the classroom teacher plays a significant role. For adults, the teacher is the coach.

With our help, Kyle set out to find a coach. He generated a list of all of the people he knew whom he believed were strong interpersonally—the people he admired and wished he could emulate in interpersonal interactions. Next, he narrowed his list to people who would have little to gain from his either succeeding or failing in his efforts to improve his interpersonal skills. Thus, for example, he would not choose a coworker against whom he was competing for jobs. Ideally, a coach should be someone who is familiar enough with your work and profession to understand what you do, but who is also distant enough from you to be able to focus objectively on the interpersonal aspects of your behavior. Finally, we suggested to Kyle that, if there was a choice between equals, he should seek the guidance of an older rather than a younger person and that he should select someone with whom a romantic relationship was unlikely to develop.

These guidelines are based upon two well-established findings. First, as people (potential coaches) enter into their 40s and 50s, they tend to become more concerned with helping younger people in their profession, and younger people in general. During their later years, most people develop a need to help younger people—to become mentors. Mentors feel a responsibility to pass on their skills and/or support to younger colleagues. Second, especially for someone who has trouble with social relationships, creating a new relationship tends to be easier if there is little likelihood of a romantic entanglement. Remember that, developmentally, you first have to develop a nonsexual "chum" relationship before you can attempt a similar relationship with someone to whom you might be sexually attracted. The same holds true for working with coaches.

Following our guidelines, Kyle selected as his ideal coach a man named Marty, the senior vice president of his division, a man ten years his senior, with whom he had had a good working relationship during his thirteen years with the company. Now that he had identified a potential coach, Kyle needed to find a way to get Marty to help.

Our suggestion was for him to meet Marty for coffee during the day or for breakfast before work in the morning. In addition, we suggested that Kyle be honest and direct about his intentions by saying something like, "I have a favor that I'd like to ask. I hope it won't be an imposition. I'm just trying to improve the way I do my job and get along with people, and I was hoping that you might be able to help give me some pointers." We have found that this kind of directness usually sets people at ease and engages their natural willingness to be helpful.

Marty accepted Kyle's invitation, so they met for breakfast before work two days later. In this setting, away from the office, Kyle elaborated on what he needed from Marty. He said that he felt that there was something in his interpersonal style, in the signals that he was sending, that might be putting others off or limiting his success in his social and work relationships. He told Marty that he had been trying to work on improving these skills himself, but it was simply impossible for him to know how he came across to others. Kyle then told him—and this is a helpful bit of information—that he had begun to work with a system based on research that was developed by clinical psychologists. He went on to explain that the psychologists, specialists in interpersonal relationships, had provided him with some guidelines and materials that would help him to overcome the problems that he had been experiencing. By telling Marty that what he was doing was part of a learning program, he further legitimized his request, emphasizing his willingness to work on himself and reassuring him that the program was not coming out of left field. Kyle went on to say that the first thing the psychologists had told him was that he needed to find someone to help him whom he trusted and whom he believed to have good interpersonal skills.

At first Marty was hesitant. This is a normal response to a somewhat unusual request. People like Marty are concerned that this is a situation in which they might hurt the other person's feelings. Here is where Kyle helped his own cause. He had to give

Marty permission to tell him the truth about box three or help him to find out what might be in box four that was causing him problems. Kyle told Marty that he knew he might not want to say things about him because it might hurt his feelings, but that he *wanted* to know what Marty and others he knew felt, regardless of whether it might be initially upsetting or not. He gave Marty permission to be honest with him—to be an interpersonal mirror. In essence, Kyle asked Marty to be his partner—his chum, but in adult terms. After considerable thought, Marty agreed to act as his coach. The two of them were ready to move further into step two: identifying the problem.

Assessment Means Systematic Observation and Feedback

Having established the coaching partnership, Kyle and Marty were ready to start identifying Kyle's nonverbal shortcomings. You and your coach should devote about two weeks to this task. Kyle and his coach need to do observations, fill out questionnaires, and meet with one another to provide feedback. Just as a medical diagnosis becomes the foundation for proper treatment, the assessment process in step two is central and critical to getting you off on the right foot nonverbally.

We helped begin Kyle's assessment by sending him instructional materials that he and Marty were to use in their work together. However, you don't have to write to us to get them. The materials you need are all here within this book, and we'll show you how to use them. We have questionnaires and rating scales that are based upon the information we've passed on to you in earlier chapters regarding nonverbal parts of speech, stages of relationships, and the understanding and remediation of dyssemia. The questionnaires and scales are designed to cue you and your coach in to what you must consider when seeking to discover the sources of your interpersonal frustration and/or failure.

Some information you already know about, but some will be entirely new to you. If you and your coach have a commitment to work together, our structured approach can make up for what you may lack in background for dealing with dyssemia.

There are two different components of the systematic observations and feedback in step two. One is the job of your coach and the other is yours to do. Both include heightened awareness of nonverbal patterns and provide critically important information. Further, both sets of observations are gathered during the same two-week period, but they are done independently. We'll start with the coach because his or her observations are more systematized and because they should always be addressed first in discussions in order to avoid biasing his or her impressions. Later in the chapter we will return to Kyle and describe his part in the assessment process by examining the observations he made through his diaries.

The Coach's Role in Step Two

The coach's first task is completing the Dyssemia Rating Scale (DRS), a systematic survey of the absence or presence of difficulties in the most commonly encountered problem areas of expressive and/or receptive nonverbal sign usage. (We have provided a copy of the DRS below.) Coaches are free and even encouraged to identify any other idiosyncratic behaviors that they may be aware of that are not included in the basic scale.

Kyle gave Marty a copy of the DRS and asked him to observe his behavior carefully for about two weeks. To be sure, there were probably some items on it that Marty could rate immediately (these would be box-three patterns that he already knew about as a result of prior interactions). Nevertheless, we believe the two-week period is necessary to help a coach tune into nonverbal cues for which he or she now has names and to get a more reliable reading of the partner's behavior. In this manner, information that might have fallen into box four at the start of the observation could be moved quickly into and through box three on its way to box one.

Take a look at the DRS with us and note the behaviors that are rated. If you are like most people, you will likely be clearer about how you would rate others than how you would rate yourself. This is why the first phase in the coaching process is so crucial—we are asking someone to watch us more carefully and in a more directed manner than before. To be sure, early in the process Kyle reported feeling self-conscious, but as is true in most instances in which we focus on our nonverbal behavior, the self-consciousness tended to recede quickly into unawareness. This is what happened to Kyle; after a day or so of being self-conscious, he adjusted and went on in his usual manner, allowing Marty a chance to focus on the behaviors he needed to observe.

The Dyssemia Rating Scale (DRS)

Directions: Please circle the frequency of each of the following behaviors according to the four-point scale below.

0	1	2	3
Never	Rarely	Sometimes	Often
	(Once in two weeks)	(Several times each week)	(Daily or more)

Section A: Gaze and Eye Contact

0	1	2	3	Fails to look at people in conversations
0	1	2	3	Fails to look at others when speaking to groups
0	1	2	3	Avoids eye contact when walking by people
0	1	2	3	Fails to look up when addressed
0	1	2	3	Hangs head when listening to people

0 1 2 3 Stares at the floor when talking with people
0 1 2 3 Watches people out of corner of his/her eye
0 1 2 3 Stares excessively at people

A Score:_____(Max = 24)

Section B: Space and Touch

0 1 2 3 Touches people inappropriately
0 1 2 3 Stands too close to people when interacting
0 1 2 3 Stands too distant from people when interacting
0 1 2 3 Seeks excessive physical contact with people
0 1 2 3 Pulls back when approached by people
0 1 2 3 Grabs people to get their attention
0 1 2 3 Spreads materials beyond his/her "area" when working
0 1 2 3 Makes people uncomfortable with his/her physical positioning
0 1 2 3 Enters offices without knocking or seeking recognition/permission
0 1 2 3 Sits down in office without invitation to do so

B Score:_____(Max = 30)

Section C: Paralanguage

0 1 2 3 Speaks too softly to be heard easily
0 1 2 3 Speaks too loudly for situation
0 1 2 3 Uses vocabulary inappropriate to listeners or situation
0 1 2 3 Tone of voice does not fit emotional state
0 1 2 3 Tone of voice does not fit situation
0 1 2 3 Mumbles when speaking
0 1 2 3 Speaks in a monotone

0 1 2 3 Speaks with "baby talk"
0 1 2 3 Fails to alter speech volume to fit situation

C Score:_____(Max = 27)

Section D: Facial Expression

0 1 2 3 Facial expressions do not fit emotional state
0 1 2 3 Uses inappropriate facial expressions
0 1 2 3 Face is blank when discussing emotional topics
0 1 2 3 Usual resting facial expression is negative (e.g., sad or angry)
0 1 2 3 Does not smile back when smiled at
0 1 2 3 Looks disinterested or bored
0 1 2 3 Facial expressions are hard to read
0 1 2 3 Facial expressions are exaggerated

D Score:_____(Max = 24)

Section E: Objectics (Fashion)

0 1 2 3 Shows inadequate personal hygiene
0 1 2 3 Shows inadequate grooming (e.g., hair uncombed, teeth uncared for)
0 1 2 3 Clothing appears uncared for
0 1 2 3 Clothing inappropriate for situation (over- or underdressed)
0 1 2 3 Uses excessive perfume or cologne
0 1 2 3 Uses poor manners when eating or drinking
0 1 2 3 Seems unaware of styles within peer group
0 1 2 3 Choice of accessories (e.g., jewelry) provokes undue negative attention

E Score:_____(Max = 24)

Section F: Hands and Hand Gestures

0 1 2 3 Hands give off nervousness or confusion
0 1 2 3 Hand gestures are too intense for situation
0 1 2 3 Fidgets with rings or other jewelry; plays with pens or pencils
0 1 2 3 Cracks knuckles when with others or drums fingers unconsciously
0 1 2 3 Hides hands in pockets or behind back
0 1 2 3 Does not attend to grooming of hands and fingernails
0 1 2 3 Hand gestures are poorly timed with speech content

F Score:_____(Max = 21)

Section G: Social Rules/Norms

0 1 2 3 Has difficulty understanding social rules and etiquette
0 1 2 3 Makes embarrassing behavioral mistakes
0 1 2 3 Lacks common sense in peer interactions
0 1 2 3 Seems tactless
0 1 2 3 Has difficulty saying funny things or telling jokes successfully
0 1 2 3 Seems to lack social maturity
0 1 2 3 Does not seem to follow office or professional etiquette
0 1 2 3 Raises conversation topics out of nowhere

G Score:_____(Max = 24)

Section H: Nonverbal Receptivity

0 1 2 3 Misreads the intentions or feelings of others
0 1 2 3 Perseveres in action or comments regardless of adverse impact
0 1 2 3 Seems insensitive to others' feelings
0 1 2 3 Seems hypersensitive to others' feelings
0 1 2 3 Behavior is out of synch with demands of situation
0 1 2 3 Fails to respond appropriately (or at all) to greetings
0 1 2 3 Doesn't seem to sense interpersonal trouble
0 1 2 3 Appears unaware of things going on around him/her
0 1 2 3 Does not check his/her appearance in mirrors or in window reflections

H Score:_____(Max = 27)

Section I: Conversational Skills

0 1 2 3 Starts talking before others finish
0 1 2 3 Does not read cues regarding desire of other people to converse or not
0 1 2 3 Does not pick up "your turn" signals
0 1 2 3 Speaks too fast for situation
0 1 2 3 Speaks to slowly for situation
0 1 2 3 Uses "y'know" or other noncontributing phrases excessively
0 1 2 3 Doesn't seem to listen to what others are saying
0 1 2 3 Choice of conversation topics is inappropriate to situation

I Score:_____(Max = 24)

Section J: Chronemics and the Use of Time

0 1 2 3 Arrives late for meetings
0 1 2 3 Leaves meetings too early or at inappropriate times
0 1 2 3 Stays well beyond time needed to complete business
0 1 2 3 Walks too fast for situation
0 1 2 3 Walks too slowly for situation
0 1 2 3 Does not wait appropriate amounts of time for people
0 1 2 3 Finishes eating long after or long before others
0 1 2 3 Makes people feel pressured to move more quickly
0 1 2 3 Checks time too frequently
0 1 2 3 Bolts to leave as soon as workday is over

J Score:_____(Max = 30)

Total Score (Sum of scores on A–J):_____(Max = 254)

For the two weeks following their initial meeting, Marty kept track of Kyle's interpersonal behavior. Having read over the DRS, he had become more and more sensitized to the sorts of behaviors for which he should be watching. At the end of the two weeks, Marty completed the DRS for Kyle and was ready to meet with him to discuss his findings. In terms of our remediation process, he had the information that they needed for step two. We will use Marty's observations of Kyle in the following scale as an example of how we score the scale and how we use its results.

Kyle's Profile on the Dyssemia Rating Scale (DRS)

Directions: Please circle the frequency of each of the following behaviors according to the four point scale below.

0	1	2	3
Never	Rarely	Sometimes	Often
	(Once in two weeks)	(Several times each week)	(Daily or more)

Section A: Gaze and Eye Contact

0 1 (2) 3 Fails to look at people in conversations
0 1 (2) 3 Fails to look at others when speaking to groups
0 1 (2) 3 Avoids eye contact when walking by people
(0) 1 2 3 Fails to look up when addressed
(0) 1 2 3 Hangs head when listening to people
0 (1) 2 3 Stares at the floor when talking with people
(0) 1 2 3 Watches people out of corner of his/her eye
(0) 1 2 3 Stares excessively at people

A Score: 7 (Max = 24)

Section B: Space and Touch

(0) 1 2 3 Touches people inappropriately
0 1 2 (3) Stands too close to people when interacting
(0) 1 2 3 Stands too distant from people when interacting
(0) 1 2 3 Seeks excessive physical contact with people
0 (1) 2 3 Pulls back when approached by people
(0) 1 2 3 Grabs people to get their attention
0 1 (2) 3 Spreads materials beyond his/her "area" when working
0 1 (2) 3 Makes people uncomfortable with his/her physical positioning

0 1 (2) 3 Enters offices without knocking or seeking recognition/permission
0 (1) 2 3 Sits down in office without invitation to do so

B Score: 10 (Max = 30)

Section C: Paralanguage

(0) 1 2 3 Speaks too softly to be heard easily
(0) 1 2 3 Speaks too loudly for situation
(0) 1 2 3 Uses vocabulary inappropriate to listeners or situation
0 (1) 2 3 Tone of voice does not fit emotional state
0 1 (2) 3 Tone of voice does not fit situation
(0) 1 2 3 Mumbles when speaking
(0) 1 2 3 Speaks in a monotone
(0) 1 2 3 Speaks with "baby talk"
0 (1) 2 3 Fails to alter speech volume to fit situation

C Score: 4 (Max = 27)

Section D: Facial Expression

(0) 1 2 3 Facial expressions do not fit emotional state
0 (1) 2 3 Uses inappropriate facial expressions
0 1 (2) 3 Face is blank when discussing emotional topics
(0) 1 2 3 Usual resting facial expression is negative (e.g., sad or angry)
(0) 1 2 3 Does not smile back when smiled at
0 1 (2) 3 Looks disinterested or bored
0 1 (2) 3 Facial expressions are hard to read
(0) 1 2 3 Facial expressions are exaggerated

D Score: 7 (Max = 24)

Section E: Objectics (Fashion)

(0)	1	2	3	Shows inadequate personal hygiene
(0)	1	2	3	Shows inadequate grooming (e.g., hair uncombed, teeth uncared for)
(0)	1	2	3	Clothing appears uncared for
(0)	1	2	3	Clothing inappropriate for situation (over- or underdressed)
(0)	1	2	3	Uses excessive perfume or cologne
(0)	1	2	3	Uses poor manners when eating or drinking
(0)	1	2	3	Seems unaware of styles within peer group
(0)	1	2	3	Choice of accessories (e.g., jewelry) provokes undue negative attention

E Score: __0__ (Max = 24)

Section F: Hands and Hand Gestures

0	1	(2)	3	Hands give off nervousness or confusion
0	(1)	2	3	Hand gestures are too intense for situation
0	(1)	2	3	Fidgets with rings or other jewelry; plays with pens or pencils
0	1	(2)	3	Cracks knuckles when with others or drums fingers unconsciously
(0)	1	2	3	Hides hands in pockets or behind back
(0)	1	2	3	Does not attend to grooming of hands and fingernails
(0)	1	2	3	Hand gestures are poorly timed with speech content

F Score: __6__ (Max = 21)

Section G: Social Rules/Norms

0	1	(2)	3	Has difficulty understanding social rules and etiquette
(0)	1	2	3	Makes embarrassing behavioral mistakes
0	(1)	2	3	Lacks common sense in peer interactions
0	(1)	2	3	Seems tactless
0	1	(2)	3	Has difficulty saying funny things or telling jokes successfully
(0)	1	2	3	Seems to lack social maturity
0	(1)	2	3	Does not seem to follow office or professional etiquette
0	(1)	2	3	Raises conversation topics out of nowhere

G Score: 8 (Max = 24)

Section H: Nonverbal Receptivity

(0)	1	2	3	Misreads the intentions or feelings of others
(0)	1	2	3	Perseveres in action or comments regardless of adverse impact
(0)	1	2	3	Seems insensitive to others' feelings
(0)	1	2	3	Seems hypersensitive to others' feelings
(0)	1	2	3	Behavior is out of synch with demands of situation
0	(1)	2	3	Fails to respond appropriately (or at all) to greetings
(0)	1	2	3	Doesn't seem to sense interpersonal "trouble"
0	(1)	2	3	Appears unaware of things going on around him/her
(0)	1	2	3	Does not check his/her appearance in mirrors or in window reflections

H Score: 2 (Max = 27)

Section I: Conversational Skills

0 1 2 3 Starts talking before others finish
0 1 2 3 Does not read cues regarding desire of other people to converse or not
0 1 2 3 Does not pick up "your turn" signals
0 1 2 3 Speaks too fast for situation
0 1 2 3 Speaks to slowly for situation
0 1 2 3 Uses "y'know" or other noncontributing phrases excessively
0 1 2 3 Doesn't seem to listen to what others are saying
0 1 2 3 Choice of conversation topics is inappropriate to situation

I Score: __4__ (Max = 24)

Section J: Chronemics and the Use of Time

0 1 2 3 Arrives late for meetings
0 1 2 3 Leaves meetings too early or at inappropriate times
0 1 2 3 Stays well beyond time needed to complete business
0 1 2 3 Walks too fast for situation
0 1 2 3 Walks too slowly for situation
0 1 2 3 Does not wait appropriate amounts of time for people
0 1 2 3 Finishes eating long after or long before others
0 1 2 3 Makes people feel pressured to move more quickly
0 1 2 3 Checks time too frequently
0 1 2 3 Bolts to leave as soon as workday is over

J Score: __0__ (Max = 30)

Total Score (Sum of scores on A–J): __46__ (Max = 254)

Once his systematic observation has been completed, the coach is ready to move to the second part of step two. Here he provides feedback and the partners begin identifying patterns and problems in nonverbal language. In fact, both your coach's materials and your own diaries will be available when you sit down for this part of the assessment, but for ease of discussion, we'll discuss them separately right now.

Let's begin with Kyle's DRS. First, we need to give you some sense of what the various scores mean. In our experience, people who have little or no evidence of dyssemia will score extremely low on the DRS. How low is low? Scores of 2 or less on the individual scales (A through J) and of 8 or less on the total score. Scores of 3 to 6 on any of the A to J scales merit your attention to that area. Should your overall score be somewhere between 15 and 25, then there is an indication of a moderate dyssemia. If your scores overall are above 25, you probably are dyssemic and it is making your life difficult. Being organized as it is, the DRS helps us (and others) focus in on the areas in which:

1. there may be a problem in nonverbal language use; and
2. correction may be needed and beneficial.

Kyle's profile suggests that both of these conditions apply in this case.

Gaze and Eye Contact

In section A, dealing with gaze and eye contact, Marty noted that Kyle does not look at other people when interacting with them. It seems that he avoids eye contact not only in individual conversations, but in groups as well. In fact, even in casual moments, Kyle fails to look at people. However, this difficulty is offset by the positive observations that Kyle is attentive when addressed and does not stare at people. According to these findings, Kyle needs to work on his eye contact, a fairly simple deficit to remediate, but one with serious implications for ongoing interpersonal interactions.

How important is eye contact? In a series of studies, we tried to determine the most important characteristics of people who were and were not considered to be interpersonally successful. We studied children and adults of all different age groups. Our results were remarkably consistent. The top two characteristics of interpersonally skilled people were always the same: They smiled, and they looked in other people's eyes when interacting with them.

Space and Touch

Kyle needs work on smiling and establishing eye contact, but what about his use of personal space and touch? Notice that he received a score of 10. Because this is his highest subscale score, we want to give it special attention. Examination of the specific pattern of behaviors observed by Marty reveals that the only score of 3 came when he rated Kyle's tendency to stand too close to others when interacting. Kyle is a space invader. This is confirmed by the high rating for "spreading into other people's area" and the fact that his positioning vis-à-vis others sometimes makes them uncomfortable. Kyle's trouble with personal space does not seem to be related, as it often can be, to problems with touching others inappropriately. Kyle presents us with a circumscribed dyssemia to remedy: the interpersonal distance he sets between himself and others is usually too small for the situation. He stands too close to others and makes them uncomfortable. As a result, they tend to either move away from or avoid him.

The news is not all bad for Kyle. He has a problem with space usage but not touch. Violation of space rules, you will recall, tends to make people uncomfortable, but violation of touch rules can actually frighten people or may even lead them to file reports of harassment or unwelcome sexual advances. The space problem is readily correctable with some practice that we will describe in the next chapter.

By the way, the "quick start" instructions for problems with touch are relatively straightforward: In American culture, if you do not know the subtle rules regarding touch, don't touch anyone, anywhere, at any time. If you have doubts, it's better not to touch another person. These quick-start instructions point out the importance of culture in nonverbal behavior, because this would be the worst advice we could give if Kyle were living in Italy or many other more touch-oriented countries.

Paralanguage

In contrast to the problems we found in the first two sections, Kyle seems to do quite well paralinguistically. The only item Marty noted was that Kyle's tone of voice sometimes does not match the situation. While this is worth discussing, it's doubtful that it is a source for significant difficulty. Kyle simply needs to be made aware of the fact that though he is a clear speaker and does not push others away with his choice and use of words, his voice needs to be better modulated to fit different situations. Knowing the importance of paralanguage—remember that it is one of the core nonverbal skills—we can see that Marty's observations are good news for Kyle.

Facial Expressions

The good news of paralanguage doesn't carry over into the critically important area of facial expression. You may recall that that facial expression is second only to paralanguage in terms of nonverbal importance. Thus, even a small problem in using facial expressions is meaningful. Marty noted that Kyle sometimes looked disinterested or bored. The reason for this expression needs to be established. The first possibility is that Kyle may in fact be disinterested and bored much of the time. Marty's conversation with Kyle, however, revealed just the opposite. Kyle was a man who was interested in all kinds of things and was rarely if ever bored. That leaves the second and potentially more socially damaging reason: Kyle's bored resting face was incongruent with how he really was feeling. Here was a definite and significant target for correction!

Marty noted further that Kyle's face was sometimes difficult to read in ongoing interactions. Kyle often had a blank face even when talking about emotional topics. The reasons for Kyle's lack of expression are irrelevant at this point. The fact is that other people have trouble interacting with Kyle because they do not know how he is feeling.

Think about this for a moment. Most of us are brought up to try to consider and be sensitive to the needs of those around us. This is what is called common courtesy. In Kyle, however, we have a person who is hard to help out. Because he fails to express what he feels in appropriate social situations, others do not know how to respond. Imagine Kyle feeling depressed and wishing that someone would respond by trying to cheer him up. If he doesn't express his feelings of depression in his facial expression, how are others going to give him what he wants and needs? Because Kyle is unaware that he is failing to express his inner feelings, he is more prone to make mistakes in interpreting others' reactions to him. Marty has discovered a key area for Kyle to work on.

Fashion

Like paralanguage, the use of fashion cues (objectics) is a source of nonverbal strength for Kyle. This is reassuring to us for a number of reasons. First of all, it means that Marty is taking careful notes and rating each area of nonverbal processing separately. He does not feel as though he had to find some nonverbal difficulty when there isn't one there. Second, it means that Kyle has another area of strength in his nonverbal repertoire.

Look for a moment at items listed under the "Fashion" heading. These are some of the most basic requirements necessary for people to achieve public acceptance in our society. We expect others to be able to care for themselves physically, to show other people the courtesy and consideration of being clean and well groomed. For a highly social society such as ours to function effectively, we must accommodate one another's most basic needs. People who have adverse ratings on objectics are typically in more serious trouble socially than many of the others we have worked with because people tend to avoid those who look unkempt or slovenly. We don't fantasize about having dinner with or doing business with someone who has not washed or is wearing soiled clothing.

Hands and Hand Gestures

Kyle has problems in using his hands to communicate. Marty noted that Kyle has "nervous" hands. Typically, we are made uncomfortable around people who wring their hands or fidget with them. While we can never really know exactly why another person is drumming his or her fingers or popping his or her knuckles, we usually assume one of a number of negative messages. We might, for example, think that the person is not trustworthy and that his or her deviousness is leaking out. Or, we might interpret the behavior as a sign of impatience with us and try to speed up our conversation or actions—or, conversely, we may get aggravated at being pressed. Alternatively, we might believe that the other person is uncomfortable with us and wants to escape.

Whatever our interpretation, the impact of nervous hands is usually adverse. Kyle's habit of finger-drumming belies his effort to appear witty and urbane. Remember that because we tend to see nonverbal signs as less consciously controllable, when words and nonverbal messages disagree, the latter overrides the former. No matter what Kyle seems to be saying verbally, his fingers communicate that he is insecure, detached, and unaware of his impact on others. Here is another prime area for improvement.

Social Norms

Marty's ratings also indicate that Kyle tends to have difficulty understanding social rules and etiquette, that he sometimes seems to lack common sense in his interactions, and that he has problems in communicating in a humorous way, despite feeling that he has a fair sense of humor. Part of the problem here may be that Kyle has simply not been taught the social graces. If this is the case, some time spent reading books like Miss Manners or Emily Post might serve him well. However, the implication that he lacks social common sense is probably the more important observation here. A lack of common sense and social know-how does not make for a pleasant social partner.

It has been our experience that common sense can be a handy interpersonal barometer of interpersonal success. The French have a phrase for common sense, *savoir faire* (literally, knowing what to do), and achieving it requires receptive nonverbal skills in voices and faces, the objectics of situations, hand positions, postures, and gestures. Thus, dyssemic problems in one or several of these nonverbal channels can ultimately manifest themselves as problems in following social norms. When Marty identified social-norm problems in Kyle, he was locking onto one of the outcomes of Kyle's multiple dyssemias.

Receptive Nonverbal Language Skills

In addition to the expressive skills needed to make any interpersonal relationship work well, receptive skills are also critical. These are assessed in section H of the DRS. Kyle's score of 2 suggests that this is not a weak area for him. There is some indication that he doesn't always respond appropriately to greetings or seem aware of what is going around him, but these minor difficulties can be easily addressed, leaving Kyle's receptive skills relatively strong.

As you will see, Kyle's having strong receptive skills will be of great potential benefit to him in his efforts to improve. In fact, we can say in general that correction of expressive dyssemias is much easier when receptive problems are absent. There are two reasons for this. First, with intact receptive skills, you can tell that something is wrong with your ongoing interactions by the negative cues you can read in the nonverbal communications of others. Second, if you can accurately read the nonverbal cues of others, you can become aware of your own expressive nonverbal inaccuracies by having the opportunity to hear and view videotapes of yourselves.

Conversational Skills

The ratings of Kyle's conversational skills reflect another area of mild concern. Marty has noticed something that we saw when we first met Kyle in the introduction: Kyle sometimes does not attend to cues as to whether or not other people want to engage in a conversation with him. As a result, he sometimes may offend people who want to talk with him by not responding appropriately. On the others side of things, Kyle might start conversations with people who are giving clear signals that they don't want to talk with him at that time.

The other DRS indicator Marty noted was that when Kyle did engage in conversations, he often chose topics that were inappropriate to the situation. Recall that when Kyle struck up an unwanted conversation with Ruth and Rosita in the opening example, he tried to talk about the Chicago Cubs, a topic that was not appropriate to a hurried work environment where people were trying to stay on task.

The rest of the ratings of Kyle's conversational skills were good. He seems not to have trouble in picking up "your turn" cues and seems to speak at an effective conversational speed. Further, his conversations are not hampered by verbal dysfluencies such as "y'know," "like," and similar nonmeaningful words or sounds. Finally—and this is critical to good conversational skills—Kyle is a good listener.

Chronemics and the Use of Time

Kyle may have a number of areas of nonverbal language that need correcting, but his use of and awareness of time is not one of them. As you can see, Marty did not find a single instance of Kyle's having any problem with chronemics. However, since some of you may have problems in this area, we'll say a few things about time usage here. Recall that chronemics is a diffuse channel of nonverbal language. This means that its impact is very general and pervasive. Further, its very pervasiveness means that the impact of chronemic dyssemia is broad and very hard to pin down.

On the DRS, we have isolated several ways in which expressive or receptive chronemic dyssemia can be manifested. One expression is seen in chronic lateness for meetings or appointments and inability to judge the proper amount of time to wait for someone or have someone wait for you. Another is moving too fast or too slow for the people you are with or the situation you are in. Thirdly, we can see that excessive time sensitivity (watch-checking, bolting from work as soon as the normal day is over, without regard to special circumstances) can also communicate the wrong thing. Finally, any behavior that can create an adverse feeling of time pressure in others can be considered a form of chronemic dyssemia.

While Kyle did not have any problems with time, we urge you and your coach to take this area very seriously and carefully assess it. The misuse and misunderstanding of time, we have found, is often one of the most powerful negative forces in our relationship failures. The fact that, once identified, it is relatively easy to fix argues for working on this most important area very early in any remediation effort.

The Partner's Role in Step Two

Having looked in while Marty gave feedback to Kyle, let's return to Kyle's part in step two: identifying the problem. Remember that while Marty was doing his observations and completing the DRS, Kyle was also looking into boxes two and four to see what he could find to help himself out of his interpersonal dead end.

While Marty was spending two weeks observing him, Kyle was also hard at work. Using the materials we sent him, Kyle, was engaged in extensive self-observation. Kyle is the only one with access to information in box two, information that is known to him, but not known to others. Box two information can be as crucial to successful improvement as are accurate observations from one's coach. Focusing on our own nonverbal behavior and writing about it helps to sensitize us to what we, and others, may really be communicating.

Becoming More Aware of Your Nonverbal Cues

Try this. Close your eyes and describe to yourself the clothing you are wearing right now. Are all the buttons buttoned? All the zippers fully zipped? Are there scuffs on your shoes? Are your shoes tied well? Are there any food stains on your shirt or blouse? Are there any threads hanging from your clothing. Is your hair completely in place? Is there any remnant of food from a past meal still stuck in your teeth? Are your glasses (if you wear them) completely clean? No spots or smears? Are there any marks on the *back* of your shirt or blouse? Is your shirt or blouse tucked in front? How about in back?

We could go on and become more detailed, but here's our point. Did you not find that you gained a better sense of your impact on others by focusing specifically on these parts of your presentation? Do you feel more or less confident? Now pay some slight attention to how you feel about the things we just examined as you continue to read. If you are like most people, you will be aware of them all—every stain, scuff, or thread—for a while, but within a few minutes you will go back to being basically oblivious to them. To remind ourselves of how we look, most of us have come down to a major check when we dress in the morning and several mini-checks in front of washroom mirrors or store windows as we progress through our day.

Asking ourselves to observe what we do can reveal much useful social information. By committing himself to complete a daily diary for two weeks, Kyle began to pay attention to even the shortest interactions that he had. By paying attention, he became aware of many aspects of his style that had been previously hidden from him. In his daily diary, Kyle focused on the sorts of things that we know can be marks of dyssemia or the kinds of interpersonal difficulties that might be related to them. Now let's take a look at one of Kyle's fourteen daily records. His daily records contributed greatly to his and Marty's effort to identify areas for improvement, using the methods that we will describe later in step three. Take a moment to read over the diary entries, then follow along with us as we describe how we suggested that he—and, by extension, you—could use this information.

Kyle's Interactional Diary

Name: Kyle Date: January 17

Note each minor and major interaction that you had during the day. Record the people involved, the circumstances, and the general flavor of the conversation, and note how you felt after it ended.

1. Stopped for gas at Quik-Trip at 8 A.M. Filled tank. Man at next pump said "Good morning." I tried to say something witty like, "It would be nicer if these gas prices weren't so high!" but I stumbled on the words "gas prices." I think the guy thought I was stupid. I hated that. I went inside to pay. The cashier said something to me, but I was reading the headline on the newspaper, about the NFL playoff. I said, "Huh?" He looked at me and said, "Will there be anything else?" slowly and in a condescending way. The day has just started and I feel bad already.

2. Arrived at work. Said "Good morning" to the information clerk near the elevators. She smiled and said "Good morning" back, but she says that to everyone. I waited for the elevator and watched the floor numbers descend. Did not talk with anyone. As I got on the elevator, I smiled and said "Good morning" to several peo-

ple that I see every day. Entered office, walked past Brenda, the receptionist. She always says "Good morning" in a bright way, and I felt good saying hello to her. Passed several people in the hallway and tried to say something funny about the upcoming NFL game. I really did not want to get into a conversation because I had a lot to catch up on, so I just went on to my office. I went in and closed the door and got to work.

3. Lunch. I prefer to eat lunch at my desk so I can keep working. Besides, eating out is always stressful for me. Jan knocked on my door at 11:30 and asked if I wanted to go to lunch with her and two other people in my section. I said, "Sure," but I really did not want to go. She asked if I had any preference. I said, "No, wherever you guys want to go is fine with me." I always say this with a big smile on my face and it is never true. They always pick places I don't like, but I go anyway and have a crappy lunch. This is what happened today. They picked a Mexican place. I hate Mexican food. But I went, aggravated with myself about not saying that either I didn't want to go or I'd prefer a different place. I wish I were more assertive.

4. Afternoon uneventful. Worked. Got a Coke at 3:00. I tried to strike up a short conversation with Rosita by the Coke machine. I told her that I thought her dress looked nice. She thanked me, but I think I made her uncomfortable. I asked Ruth about the new program she had worked on, and jokingly asked her if she could get back to cooking for her husband now that the project was done. I don't think she got the joke. I felt bad and said something lame like, "Well, enough good times.

I've got to get back to solving the problems of the world." I went to my office and closed the door. People tend not to bother me when my door is closed. I'm comfortable with that. I notice that at various times during the afternoon, conversations take place in the hall. People chatting, laughing. Then it gets quiet again and people go back to work. I am definitely not good at that kind of small talk.

5. Left the office at 5:00. Needed to stop at market on the way home. Went to the Publix near my house. Met someone from church in the parking lot and walked in with him. He asked me if I was going to the retreat over the weekend. I bumbled my words again while trying to make a witty reply, saying something like, "I think I'm going to retreat from the retreat and stay at home." I thought that would be funny, but it wasn't. I felt bad as soon as I said it. He said something nice like, "Well, we'll miss you," but I couldn't believe he really meant it. We got our baskets and went our separate ways. I felt bad again.

6. Spent the evening at home. Called my sister and chatted for a while. Her family is fine. Wrote a bunch of e-mails. Ordered some books and CDs from Amazon. Watched *The West Wing* on TV. My God, this is really a boring life I'm leading here. When I write this down, it worries me. Watched the news and a little of Letterman. Another exciting day in the life of Kyle!

What Kyle and Marty (and We) Learned in Step Two

While most of us would like to believe that our lives are a never-ending whirl of fascinating and exciting events, the truth is that if we write down our activities, the vast majority of them are actually simple and mundane. We eat, we work, we shop, we visit with people, and we spend some time alone. As we look at the sample of Kyle's day, we can see that Kyle also has a fairly routine schedule and that he seems basically satisfied with his work pattern. However, several times during the day, Kyle noted that he felt bad after interactions with other people. Further, you may have noticed that these bad feelings usually came when he was judging himself after he had tried to make a witty or funny comment to someone and it had fallen flat. We also noticed that Kyle tended to avoid people if he possibly could. He was certainly polite and civil with them, but he did not report going out of his way to talk with others. His interaction with his church friend was totally accidental and probably unavoidable. He never initiated social interaction. Jan came and sought him out for lunch, perhaps to be nice and to try to pull him out of his office.

Let's apply what we know about interpersonal theory to Kyle's behavior. Remember what you learned about locus of control? Based on his diary, do you think that Kyle is more likely to be internal or external? Does he feel that what happens to him is a result of his own doing or the result of luck or fate or other people's power? Our bet is that he is externally controlled. In fact, Kyle's answers to our locus of control scale gave him a score of 14, which shows that he is indeed external compared to other adults his age. He feels relatively helpless in interpersonal situations. Being externally controlled increases the chances that he will feel anxious and depressed.

Based on his writing, Kyle sees himself and his life as boring. He believes that no one would really care about where he would want to go to lunch. Even though he wants relationships with others very much, Kyle has come to see himself as a person who is alone most of the time and who often resists the efforts of other people to pull him in. He was asked to lunch and begrudgingly agreed; he was asked about the church retreat and gave a contrived reason for not going. Note that he did not have anything else to do. Kyle is so uncomfortable around other people that he would rather not be with them. His only effort to relate to others seems to be in the form of his attempts to be funny or witty, and these efforts, in his judgment, typically fall flat. However, since attempted humor is Kyle's primary mode of interacting with people and he knows no other, he typically resorts to his hapless witticisms whenever he is with people, reinforcing his self-perception that he is a loser.

But we know a bit more about Kyle than he reports in his diaries. When we were first introduced to him in the introduction, we found that he tended to aggravate others by his remarks. His colleagues tended to avoid him. Even though Kyle feels he is friendly and uses friendly words, others are responding to him as though he is hostile. How can this be? We bet you know how we're going to explain this seeming mystery, because we are going to use a basic truth about verbal and nonverbal behavior that we have repeated often. The truth is that though Kyle describes himself as friendly and uses friendly words, there is something in the tone of his voice and in his other nonverbal expressions that produces discomfort, even anger in others. When words are friendly and nonverbal signals are hostile, people will believe the nonverbal message.

Think also about Kyle's situation from the perspective of relationships and the four-stage model (choice, beginning, deepening, and ending) that we discussed in chapter 1. It is our sense that Kyle's biggest problem is with the beginning phase of relationships. He simply has not developed a way of communicating to others—either verbally or, more importantly, nonverbally—that he is the kind of person with whom they would like to develop a friendship. Unless Kyle can move from being a stranger to being an acquaintance, he is unlikely to ever have close friends or a close and deep relationship that would make his dream of having a family someday a reality.

A look at Kyle's DRS suggests that he lacks some of the skills necessary to begin relationships. It turns out that Kyle is hard to read and is sometimes insensitive to others' needs. Despite lacking a good sense of humor, he depends on weak witticisms as his primary modus operandi in talking with people. He simply does not seem to have the basics necessary to get a relationship off the ground. Corrective efforts should begin by focusing on improving Kyle's ability to begin relationships.

The Culmination of Step Two: Completing the Assessment Process

It's now about three weeks after Kyle first asked Marty for his help. They have agreed to meet on a Saturday afternoon, knowing that this will be the longest meeting of the assessment. In response to Kyle's suggestion that they meet at a restaurant for lunch and then talk, Marty suggested that it might be easier for them to talk more freely and at length at his place. This was more than Kyle expected, but by now Marty had a sense of Kyle's need for help and he was willing to go a few extra steps to help out. Marty's wife, Sara, put out some sandwich makings and soft drinks. The two partners in Kyle's quest for self-understanding sat down and began work immediately, eating as they talked. Unlike at their previous meeting, each came ready with a stack of materials (the DRS, the diaries, informal observations) and with clearer expectations. Each of them was also much more nervous than they had been earlier. Marty was concerned that he might hurt Kyle's feelings. Kyle was worried that all his work could be a useless effort driven by what now seem to be the questionable notions of two psychology professors in Atlanta!

Following our advice, Kyle began by expressing his gratitude. He first thanked Marty for his time and energy and, second, reaffirmed his openness to whatever Marty had to say to him. Remember, permission must be given to someone in order to learn the contents of what is usually contained within Johari box three: information other people know about us that we don't know about ourselves. Permission given again, Kyle and Marty got down to work. Marty shared the information from the DRS. Kyle showed Marty his diaries and they read them over together and thought of how the DRS and the diaries meshed. Together, they were developing a picture of two people that seemed to be Kyle: Kyle as seen and experienced by those around him and Kyle as experienced by Kyle. As Marty read the diaries, he came to know a different Kyle than he had observed. He saw him as a well-meaning but bumbling guy who often expressed the wrong things but who didn't mean to drive others away. Kyle was actually a lonely and confused person who wanted to fit in better. Marty was reassured that he had made the right decision to be his coach.

As Kyle listened to what Marty had to tell him, he also began to feel differently. First of all, his sense of appreciation for Marty's time and effort redoubled. Marty had been willing to do for him what no one else in his past or present had done—to be direct with him. At the same time, Kyle realized that if he had not given Marty permission, none of this would have happened. He was learning about some negative characteristics in himself, but also that much of what was going wrong in his life could be corrected by him. It is important that blame not be assigned here, but *responsibility*, and with responsibility comes a realization of control—control over the good as well as the bad things that happen to us. Kyle was edging toward a most important realization that people can come to in an effort to improve their lives: *If I am doing things that make other people avoid or dislike me, I can also do things that will make them want to be around me!*

Kyle was able to see what he was doing to cause himself trouble and was ready to change things. It was time for step three: overcoming dyssemia. Here again, Kyle and Marty needed some basic knowledge—a set of skills and techniques that would help them develop an effective plan for remedying Kyle's dyssemia. In the next chapter, we will provide you, as we did Kyle, with this set of skills and techniques. You can see it as your own remediation tool kit. Later, in chapter 8, we will show you how to use these tools to develop your own specific program to help you conquer your nonverbal language difficulties and start moving from dyssemia toward eusemia.

Chapter 7

The Remediation Tool Kit

Step two—assessment—is now complete, and if all has gone well, you and your coach have identified those areas of your nonverbal language repertoire which need some practice and improvement. You are now ready for the last step, developing and implementing a plan for overcoming the dyssemias that you have discovered.

There are many ways to describe the process upon which we are about to embark. Thus far throughout the book, we have used verbs like *correct, improve, overcome,* and the like, but the word that we think describes best what we are hoping to do is *remediate.* Rooted in the word "remedy," remediation is a word that comes from the educational domain rather than the realm of treatment. It suggests, as we believe, that dyssemia is not some sort of illness, but rather a reflection of incomplete or misdirected learning of a skill—the skill of using nonverbal language effectively. It follows, then, that in order to overcome dyssemia and its ill effects, one has to set out on a program of learning and practice using methods directed at development and improvement of skills, rather than on a program of treatment or therapy. Further, the use of educational concepts also carries with it the implication of lifelong practice and refinement, and an awareness that no one will ever learn perfectly every skill in every area. With these thoughts in mind, we'll begin step three with a description of your remediation tool kit, a set of techniques that you can use (as did Kyle and Marty) to tailor a program of practice and improvement designed specifically for you.

One more thing. You may be wondering how long your remediation will take. The answer is that it depends to a great extent on the type, pattern, and extensiveness of your nonverbal problems. Sometimes simply becoming aware that you have particular nonverbal difficulties is enough for you to come up with your own ways to correct the problems. In other instances, your problems may require more time and effort, and the help of others. For most people, however, we would guess that the time frame will be measurable in months rather than weeks or years.

What follows in the remainder of this chapter is a primer on general principles of remediation and a description of some generalizable techniques that can be tailored to meet individual needs. Regardless of where you have found problems to correct, read about all of the techniques so that you can get a feel for the general principles of remediation. We'll be talking about all of them again when we rejoin Kyle and Marty in chapter 8.

Experiencing Zero Input: Sensitizing Yourself to the Importance of Nonverbal Cues

We have learned that one effective way of demonstrating the centrality of expressive and receptive use of nonverbal cues—and, incidentally, of the important social skill of maintaining eye contact—is to perform the following exercise.

You and your coach have just started the remediation process. First, engage in a conversation about a topic of your choosing. A few seconds into the conversation, and while your coach is talking, plug your ears with your fingers and look downward towards your own shoes. Finally, close your eyes. By doing this admittedly artificial thing, you essentially cut yourself off from all input. After focusing for a few seconds on this zero-state condition, unplug your ears and attend to the limits and benefits of just hearing words and voice tones. Now lift your gaze to include the hands and feet of your coach, but not his or her face. Notice how much easier is it to understand and follow the conversation? Finally, look directly at your coach's face and eyes and incorporate all of the information available during an interaction. If you are like most people, this will be a pretty convincing demonstration of the importance of looking at people when we talk with them. Further, the exercise demonstrates the importance of hand positions, gestures, body posture, facial expressions, and voice tone in the wholeness of interaction. By first blocking out all cues and then admitting them one at a time, you come to appreciate them each in their own right.

There are some other ways that you can achieve the same effect of blocking out one cue in order to make other cues louder. One is through use of paintings and photographs, and another is by using the ubiquitous television screen. First, let's talk about paintings and photos.

Paintings and Photographs as General Approaches to Remediation

Paintings are a very rich source of remediation materials for one very specific reason: They are peak stills. A *peak still* is a representation of a person or situation that has been rendered by the artist in as close to what the artist considers to be perfect form as possible. All the emotions, attitudes, and thoughts of the characters are depicted in ways that make the interpretation easy for most viewers. Think about this idea for a minute. The artist has had the time to get the facial expressions just right. The hands of the figures are exactly as desired; the postures are perfectly drawn. Now, these kinds of very clear representations of people and situations sometimes happen in real life, but they are relatively rare, and if one of the nonverbal channels is at peak (i.e., its meaning is crystal clear), it is unlikely that the others will be.

Think back to the last time you had a roll of film processed. Let's say it was from a family gathering. When you got back the prints, if you are like most people, you shuffled through them until you came upon one that "looked like everybody." This was the peak still for that group of photos. Or think of pictures of yourself. Again, most people going through a roll of photographs of themselves will say things like, "Oh that doesn't look like me," or "I look terrible there." Knowing that each photo is in fact actually what you looked like when it was taken, you can see that "looking like me" actually is a judgment of how well the photo fits some image that you have of yourself. This is another story, however. For our purposes here, we hope to give you the sense of why a painting can be very useful in learning about nonverbal language. Everything is optimally represented in a painting; everything is just as the artist wanted it. As such, people who are starting out to learn about the association between nonverbal cues and what they represent will find that looking at paintings is a great place to begin.

An example might be helpful. Look at the painting by Georges de La Tour on the following page. As you can see, it's a depiction of a group of people playing cards. When taken as a whole, it is clear that the title character, *The Cheat,* is the young man holding the card behind his back. But look at all of the other cues that are available to tell us about what is happening. Look at the eyes of the woman. Look at the hands of the other characters. Now try this. Show the painting to a friend, but hide the title and, using sticky parts of a Post-it note, cover the eyes of the woman and the card behind the back of the cheater. Ask friends to tell you what is going on in the painting. You will see that few people

Georges de la Tour, French, 1593–1652. The Cheat with the Ace of Clubs
Oil on canvas, late 1620s
38 ½ × 61 ½ inches (97.8 × 156.2 cm)
Kimbell Art Museum, Fort Worth, Texas

will now be able to read this painting accurately. Now uncover the eyes of the woman and ask again. Most people will now say that she is worried about something, or perhaps distracted or angry. However, they will still not be able to tell the entire story. Lastly, uncover the card and ask them again. Now the story is clear. All the nonverbal cues are in place to make sense out of what is going on.

In our lab at Emory, we tested people's abilities to decipher *The Cheat* as well as some other paintings. Some people could read paintings with fewer cues than others. Some people were "eye" people and could tell us an amazing amount about the characters by just seeing their eyes. Other people needed faces to understand what was happening, while others depended more on hands or context. Paintings are truly wonderful ways of entering the remediation process. People have spent centuries developing ways to represent the things that we react to on a daily basis. The only representations that seem to have changed significantly over time are fashion cues—clothes, hairstyles, and the like. A sad face painted by Rafael in the sixteenth century still produces a similar impact in the twenty-first. The smile of Leonardo daVinci's *Mona Lisa* is still enigmatic after nearly half a millennium.

There is one other critically important aspect of painting interpretation that is immensely helpful to remember both in remediation and in reading real-life situations. This is what is called in art terminology the *chorus effect*, referring to the fact that we often can learn more by looking at what is going on *around* people than by looking at people themselves—an effect that's well represented in the painting, *The Last Supper* by Leonardo. Consider all of the differences in the hand gestures, grouping, head turns, and postures in the disciples in this moment immediately after Jesus tells them that one of their number will betray him. The complexity of his feelings can only be fully understood through the variety of responses seen in the chorus.

Consider a real-life example of using the chorus effect to learn about how people feel. Imagine you are looking at a video of a woman with tears flowing down her cheeks. Her mouth is open and she is staring off to the left of the frame. All you can see is her face. What might she be feeling? Most of us would guess she is weeping and sad. Now imagine the camera pans back and we see that people on both sides of her are laughing and looking in the same direction as she is. Our guess now is that she is crying with laughter. She is at a comedy show and is looking at the stage. The chorus effect—the context, through which nonverbal cues come to us—is critical to our learning how to relate more effectively to people.

How do you and your coach find paintings to use in this way? Possibilities are all around you. Go to a museum or take a book or two out from a library and spend time with the paintings from fifteenth- through nineteenth-century Italy, France, Spain, and the Netherlands. The artists of these times made special efforts to represent both lofty and everyday situations in ways that would evoke specific emotional responses in viewers. They wrote about and practiced the production of exact facial expressions, hand gestures, and postures that would show the feelings of their characters. Their paintings are peak stills that are especially useful in the remediation of dyssemia. (A useful source of paintings can be found in the internet museums, such as www.kfki.hu/~arthp/index.html, www.artcyclopedia.com, and www.ibiblio.org/wm/.)

We'll get more specific in chapter 8, but for now, when using paintings, we suggest that you start by covering the faces of the characters. This will serve to make the other nonverbal cues "louder." (The same will be true for photos and television programs, which we will describe shortly.) Most of our students and clients have said that what they noticed first after they covered faces are the hands of the characters. They also notice how much they can learn about the painting from the hands alone. Notice what happens for you when you cover the faces of the characters. What are your own secondary "favorite" nonverbal cues?

Photographs

While paintings provide us with a wonderful source of nonverbal information, we have an even richer source that is more readily available: photographs. As we mentioned earlier, most photographs are not peak stills. Thus, from among the many photos that are taken of a particular event, we might select one or two that we believe truly capture the moment. It would not be an exaggeration to say that hundreds of thousands of photos were taken during the assassination and funeral of John F. Kennedy, yet the one photo that summed up the loss to our country and the more personal loss to his family was that of his son, little John-John, saluting as his father's casket passed.

There are two photographic sources for remediation materials:

formal photographs found in magazines and family photo albums, and informal photographs found in the usually chaotic photo collections in nearly every home across the country. Both are helpful for our purposes, but in different ways. Let's look at the first one, magazine photos and albums. These comprise photos that have been selected because they are communicating information, either intentionally or serendipitously, that is of interest to you. Thus, a photo in an advertisement, such as you might see in a fashion magazine, might depict a young woman who is happy, carefree, sexy, and likes her new handbag. The producer of the advertisement is counting on the majority of viewers getting the same message from this photo: This bag can make you look and feel like a carefree, happy, sexy person, too! Analysis of this and many other photos in advertisements can tune you in to the sorts of cues that may be close to universally understood. What holds for the advertising photo usually holds for real-life responses. If this were not true, the money spent on ads would be wasted.

Family album photos are also like the magazine photos in that they are selected because they communicate specific messages to you. They are peak stills. They show Aunt Mary as we (and, most of the time, she) would like to see her. They show Dad or Mom as we remember them or as they would like to remember themselves. They show little Brandon smiling as he rounds third after hitting a little league home run, not rounding third with his head down and his face out of sight. Album photos can help us to become aware of how people like to look and how they like other people to look and, as such, serve as a valuable indicator of the do's and don'ts of fashion, postures, gestures, and the like.

Now consider the second set of photos, the ones that were *un*selected. These are the photos that did not make the album cut. However, most people have trouble throwing away or destroying photos of themselves, or of others for whom they care. We can easily throw away a bad photo of a street scene in Chicago, but most of us would be unable to throw away a bad picture of one of our children, parents, or friends. Although these photos are relegated to the drawer because they are not quite right, they can be an incredibly valuable resource in remediation. To help develop receptive nonverbal language skills, one need only to reach into a stack of these nonpeak photos and try to analyze them for reasons they were rejected. What about the facial expression here was not optimal? Is Uncle Ned looking like he's daydreaming at his anniversary party? Is this posture the reason for the photo's rejection? Does this one make me look awkward or uncoordinated? What are the effects of a half-smile on viewers? It's a party and Bill looks miserable. Maybe that's the reason this photo is in the drawer!

With the rejected photos, you have a gold mine of information that can help you to understand why people tend to reject certain facial expressions, postures, gestures, and such in real life. Look at them with your coach. See if you can sort them into groups based upon why they were not album material. Notice which ones you have the most trouble understanding. As with the paintings, see what happens to your reaction to the people in the photos if you cover their faces. Do you have a different reaction? Learn from that observation.

Finally, look at photos of yourself. Are you like some people in that you do not like most photos taken of you? Are you always angry looking? Is your smile weak? Overdone? Remember, what you look like in the picture is actually what you looked like at the instant the photo was taken. Is that what you look like most of the time? This is very much like making you aware of your voice on a tape recorder.

Your Television Set

After the number of times that you may have been told as a child to stay away from the TV set, you will appreciate that the TV is actually a wonderful source of material for basic as well as very high-level dyssemia-remediation efforts. Compared to paintings and photographs, television is one step closer to real life. After all, paintings and photographs are static. We have time to look at them and try to decide what various nonverbal cues might mean. However, like live interactions, TV images are dynamic. They are moving and changing all the time. Some of you will be able to read nonverbal cues in static situations, but will get flustered once behavior is in motion. Any remediation effort must include practice with moving stimuli—with television and with real-live human beings.

Television shows can be used in many of the same ways as paintings and photos. Start by sitting down with your coach in front of a TV set. Find shows that have people being emotional. Soap operas are particularly good candidates. Turn off the sound but keep watching. Notice what happens? All of the other sources of information besides words and paralanguage suddenly become "louder." Facial expressions are suddenly easier to read as you begin to depend on the other sources of nonverbal information to tell you what is going on and how the people are feeling. This is akin to an ophthalmologist strengthening weak eye muscles in a child by having him or her cover the good eye with a patch, thereby forcing the bad eye to work harder. Try to identify the feelings of the characters based just on their faces. If you are working on gestures, watch only the characters' hands and arms. This is an excellent way to practice observing nonverbal behavior, and to get better at it.

You can use the TV to work on tone of voice also. Here's how. Your coach sits next to you and continues to look at the TV screen. You, however, turn your back to the screen so that the only information you get is the tone of voice of the characters. Now you have shut out all the visual cues and must depend on paralanguage. This is the same principle as the eye patch again. If you want to improve your skills at reading voice tone, block out the visual information. Describe what is going on to your coach, who is actually watching the show. Have your coach tell you when you are right and wrong. Using vocal tones, try to describe what the facial expressions, postures, and gestures of the speakers might look like.

Would you like to know why the blocking-out methods (in paintings, photos, and television shows) work so effectively? Some of you are right-handed and some left-handed. However, if an injury occurs to your preferred hand, you must depend on the other hand. You can learn to eat, wash, shave, even dress effectively, *if you have to.* Further, we have known people who, after having been forced to use their nondominant hand for a period of time, have continued to use it in some situations—sometimes even after their preferred hand was available once more.

Our research has shown us that just as people have preferred hands, they also have preferred sorts of nonverbal cues. Thus, there are people who prefer to watch others' eyes. Not surprisingly these people do not like to interact with people who are wearing sunglasses. Other people pay most attention to voice tone; still others focus most on posture. When we have a choice of which set of nonverbal cues to use during an interaction, we tend to go to our preferred way of using nonverbal information, whether it is accurate or not. But, if we are prevented from using our preferred mode, we can and do go to another nonverbal means of gathering information.

Each of us usually depends most on one or two sources of nonverbal social information. So long as that source of information is available to us *and we are in fact good at using it,* we function well. However, if either the information is not available (for example, if we depend a lot on eyes and faces we—like one of your authors—will probably do poorly in telephone conversations) or if we are, in fact, *not* really good at using our preferred cue, problems can develop in our interpersonal functioning.

The TV set can be used as a powerful remediation device here. If you want to find out what your preferred source of information is, block out one or the other of the major "parts of speech" and see when you begin to feel uncomfortable or your coach begins to tell you that you are misperceiving. Use the TV to work on your weak spots. Put a "patch" over your preferred cues and force yourself to strengthen your other skills. If you learn that you are very frequently misinterpreting one set of cues, try to stop depending on them in your interactions. We worked with a woman business executive who had a deficit in reading faces, but who was really good at reading voice tones. Awareness that she was depending on a nonverbal set of cues that she was in fact weak at reading led her to consciously depend more on what she heard than on what she saw.

The Mall

Shopping malls turn out to be a boon for those of us involved in the assessment and remediation of dyssemia. Malls attract people from all walks of life and with all sorts of moods to a central place. If there were ever a perfect place to observe nonverbal communication in action, this is it!

You and your coach should take a seat in a place that will allow you to view many people and tables. It is not necessary to hear what people are saying. The mall is an especially good place to work on what we have called the long-distance communicators, such as postures, hand positions and other gestures, objectics, touch, and space. Using nonverbal cues, you will have a chance to try and figure out what the relationships are between people and how they feel about one another. You can try to read families as they interact around their purchases. You can observe the resting facial expressions and postures of solitary eaters to see if they are positive or negative.

The Camcorder and the Cassette Recorder: Expressive Remediation

The majority of uses for paintings, photos, and television shows are in the domain of receptive dyssemias. That is, they are very helpful in teaching us to become sensitized to the box-four nonverbal cues in our environment. However, as you know, there are also expressive dyssemias, and these can require additional hardware.

If your problem is in the area of paralanguage, we suggest that you use a tape recorder since it will isolate your tone of voice more effectively. Simply turn on the tape recorder and have a conversation with your coach about some topic. Don't worry, your initial self-consciousness will soon disappear.

In addition to the conversation with your coach, also record your end of a telephone conversation. It is amazing to see how many people's voices change when they speak on the phone. Some people who are highly effective paralinguistically in person are hopeless bumblers on the phone. Finally, if oral presentations are an important part of your job, record your presentations as raw material for later analyses.

After recording yourself under different conditions, you and your coach can listen to the tapes. Attend to rate of speech, clarity of pronunciation, loudness, and tone of voice. Do you sound pleasant? Are you boring? Be honest with yourself and ask your coach for honest input. Do you remind yourself of anyone that you like to listen to? How about someone that you don't like listening to? Don't worry about feeling that the voice doesn't sound like you. The way you sound on the recorder *is* the way you sound to others. Change the way it sounds to you in such a way that it sounds better on the tape and you are getting there! Caution: This will take practice—lots of practice.

Use the camcorder when you and your coach think that you

have problems in one of the visual channels. Start out again with a conversation between you and your coach. Sit in a comfortable chair and talk to each other, not to the camera. See how you look when someone is "looking in on you." Next, have your coach have a conversation with you while he or she holds the camcorder. Look at the camera as you speak and try to converse with your coach. This is awkward at first, but it gets easier with time. Next, make a tape of yourself giving the same kind of short speech or presentation that we described when we talked about audiotaping. Stand as you would in a real presentation and actually present the material, using any props and charts that you used in the past.

Next, tape yourself walking towards and away from the camera. Tape yourself walking in front of the camera from right to left, then from left to right. This is so that you can get a look at how you walk. Now tape yourself doing some routine activities. Walk into a room, close the door. Go to a chair. Sit on the chair. Cross your legs and uncross them. Sit on a sofa. Drink some coffee. Anything that you do routinely should be examined.

Remember, a small thing can make a big difference. We had a client once whose superior was driven to distraction by the way she rinsed her mouth with her sip of coffee before swallowing it. An innocent-seeming habit, yet it was unknowingly affecting her life. Truly, in the everyday simple things, we often find some of the silliest, but also most real, reasons for our interpersonal problems.

When you have completed your videotape, sit down with your coach, or alone, and look at it *without the sound*. Be systematic in the way you use the tape. We suggest that you go through it as many times as there are areas that you want to examine. In other words, if you are looking at your posture in various situations, run the tape and look *only* at posture. Make notes for yourself. Talk over postures with your coach. Think of how you would be affected if you saw this posture in others. Continue on with repeated viewings for gestures, facial expressions, use of space, objectics, and any other channel you want to check out. This will take some time, but for the most part you are going to find out that, in fact, you look pretty good! You may come upon a few things that you'd like to work on, but if you are like most people—even most people with a dyssemia—you will be mostly A-okay nonverbally.

After playing the tape through with specific nonverbal channels in mind, observe the ways in which you differ from situation to situation. Are you stiff when speaking in front of a crowd? What happens to your body posture when you walk into a room? Do you communicate what you want to about yourself when seated? How about when you are walking? What nonverbal behavior would you like to see less of? What would you like to see more of?

Lastly, view the tape again with the sound on. This time, your purpose is different. Here you are looking for what we called congruence back in the introduction. Recall that this refers to the degree to which your verbal and nonverbal channels agree in what they are communicating. Here you will get a chance to see if your posture says that you are a ready-to-go kind of person while your voice sounds hesitant. You can see if you are constantly presenting a set of impressions that can be read clearly by others. Because they are difficult for you to see yourself, your coach will be particularly important here.

What we want to emphasize here and throughout all of our work is that you should understand and use your nonverbal behaviors in the same way that you understand and use your verbal skills. Know how to use lots of them, know how they affect other people, know which situations call for what kind of behavior, and use the most effective behavior (for you) in each situation. In other words, even if you feel uncomfortable, if a situation calls for a particular way of acting in order for others to feel comfortable and for you to succeed, you might want to choose to act that way—but you can choose *not to* as well!

Perhaps an example will help here. You know there are cultural and international differences in nonverbal language. This is relatively less true for things like tone of voice and facial expressions than it is for postures and gestures. In Great Britain, for example, it is common for males to cross their legs "knee over knee" rather than the more American "ankle over knee" cross. This difference is quite striking when you are at a meeting attended by Brits and Americans, where you can essentially divide the groups according to nationality without hearing them utter a word.

In the United States, the British style of leg crossing is not seen as "macho," and many American men may feel uncomfortable sitting in this way. On the other hand, British people tend to see the American leg-cross as a bit arrogant and impolite. The solution? When we are in Britain, we sit with our legs crossed in the knee-over-knee position. We feel a little funny about it, but our British colleagues seem to relate to us more comfortably and we get on with what we are doing very successfully. Do we have to do this? No. But given what we know about the impact of our postures, we choose to do what we can to make our relationships go smoothly. Could we choose not to accommodate? Sure! And so could you! But why?

A Final General Remediation Lesson: The Strategy of Behavioral "Borrowing"

As psychologists, we spend much of our time thinking about behavior. What intrigues us most are questions like, "Why do people act as they do?" and "Where do people's behaviors come from?" Perhaps the entire history of psychology could be distilled down to these two questions.

The most satisfying and best-documented answer to the question of behavioral sources is that we *learn* them. That is, as a result of experience, we not only add ways of acting to our behavioral repertoire, but also some sense of *when* the behavior is to be used. In the history of psychology, there were theorists who believed that people only learned behaviors when they were rewarded. Thus, the classical research in which Pavlov taught his dogs to salivate to the sound of a bell or Skinner got his rats to press a small bar in order to obtain food were thought to be the prime demonstrations of how new behaviors are instilled. However, the last century of research has shown us a new source of behavioral change called *imitation learning,* also known as *observational learning* and *vicarious learning.* All three names refer to the same fact—that we need not experience the consequences of a behavior directly in order to learn it. We can learn by watching what other people do and observing what happens to them after they do it.

As clinical psychologists trying to find ways to develop new and more effective behavior patterns, we have also found that imitation learning is a most powerful tool. It is a way for you to seek out and find behaviors that may be able to fill in the empty spaces in your own social behavioral repertoire. Via imitation learning, in other words, you can actually borrow behaviors from other people and make them your own. The difference is that rather than letting the observational learning affect you in a passive way, as is the case in the natural order of things, we suggest that you purposely and actively seek to borrow behaviors. Imagine that you need to develop a nonverbal skill. Look around for someone who seems to show that particular nonverbal skill, then borrow the behavior and make it your own.

Teaching Social Skills through Behavioral Borrowing—Seshu

We worked with a man named Seshu whose social skills were very poor. Seshu was so desperately shy and withdrawn that if people introduced themselves to him he would not even state his name in return! This is what happened when we first met Seshu:

Steve: Hi, I'm Steve Nowicki. Nice to meet you.
Seshu: Hi.

Seshu completely missed the cues in Steve's introduction that say to most of us, "OK, now you say your name!" If you met Seshu you would judge him to be awkward at best, and at worst very strange. Seshu did not even know the basics of social introduction. He had a long way to go. Seshu's remediation began with behavioral borrowing. We asked him to bring us a tape of a television character who, he felt, had good social skills. We reserved the right to disagree if we felt he had chosen a poor model. He chose Frazier, the fictional on-air psychiatrist who, although a bit frazzled at times, certainly seems to know how to talk to people. We watched the *Frazier* tape with Seshu and isolated a couple of instances in which the character met people and said, "Hi, I'm Frazier Crane." After playing the tapes, we asked Seshu to try to imitate Frazier's style, voice tone, and movements. The results were remarkable. Once we got him to stop calling himself "Frazier Crane" and use his own name, he felt that he had added an important skill to his repertoire. In the days to follow, he used his *Frazier* style several times and people responded well to him. A successful behavioral transfer had occurred.

Seshu's problems were fundamental. He needed to borrow many behaviors even to be able to get past the rudimentary beginnings of a relationship. For example, we have found that people who are having relationship troubles at work can benefit immensely from borrowing from people who have already succeeded at doing what they want to do. One such person was Mandy, a thirty-two-year-old account executive with a firm specializing in internal communications.

Advanced-Level Behavioral Borrowing—Mandy

Mandy was a graduate of an excellent northeastern college and had majored in public relations and marketing. She was well prepared to work in an industry specializing in communication among employees in large corporations. Her CEO had great hopes for her, but about six months into her job, it was clear that Mandy lacked some essential "closing" skills. She could make wonderful proposals and presentations, but when it came to getting clients to sign on, she had special trouble. We saw Mandy on referral from her CEO.

Mandy was the perfect client for us. She was bright, achievement-oriented, and willing to try anything to improve her abilities and status at work. The solution turned out to be simple: behavioral borrowing. We advised Mandy to ask several of the other account execs to allow her to accompany them when they did presentations and closed on deals. Mandy's task was to find the one among the three she observed who did things in a way that impressed her most. Having made this selection, Mandy carefully analyzed what her colleague did and said, how she sat, how she looked. She then practiced with us, adopting her borrowed style. We felt it was important for us to see and react to the style so that we could feel secure (1) that she indeed was acting differently, and (2) that she did not borrow any behaviors that might not "fit." (An example that comes to mind here is a woman who used a male as a role model and tried to borrow his greatly outsized handshake. It worked for him. It definitely did not work for her!)

Over the course of her next three job presentations, Mandy used her new style. It was awkward at first—unless you feel awkward you're probably not doing anything differently!—but soon it became second nature. It was most effective and we are pleased to report that she is now a vice president with her company.

• • •

Research on imitation learning also has shown clearly that not only do we learn what works, but what doesn't work as well. Imagine a student in one of our classes, for example, coming up to ask a question and receiving a highly audible answer like, "That is the most ridiculous thing I have ever heard. You most definitely cannot take the final exam early!" Few other students, if any, would come up and ask the same question, even though none of them had actually experienced the consequence. A dyssemic student, on the other hand, might just be the exception!

What we have tried to do in this chapter is to introduce you to some general methods for the remediation of dyssemia. With the basic tool kit we have given you, we believe that it will be possible for you and your coach to develop all sorts of creative remediation activities. Armed with the general guidelines presented here, let's move forward to the next and final chapter, where we end our journey. We will rejoin Kyle's remediation in progress, where we will transform our general principles of remediation into more specific ones.

Chapter 8

Developing Your Remediation Plan

By going through their Dyssemia Rating Scales and Kyle's self-generated diaries, Kyle and Marty have moved as much information as possible into box one. What was known by each is now known by both. They also had learned about the tool kit that we described in the last chapter and were aware that each person's remediation program must be tailored to fit his or her needs. Therefore, Kyle and Marty developed a set of exercises and activities directed specifically at the receptive and expressive deficits they had identified. Here in this chapter, we want to show you how you and your coach can do this by providing examples from Kyle's remediation programs, as well as several other people's.

In the next section, we will go through each of the areas focused upon in the DRS and describe how the basic tools can be applied more specifically. In addition, we will also present specific techniques that have been devised for redressing specific areas of need. Again, we want to emphasize that each and every one of the remediation techniques can be modified by you and your coach in order to accommodate your specific situation.

Remediating Problems in Gaze and Eye Contact

By now you know how important eye contact is in the formula for social success. Poor eye contact is a very frequent problem in people with dyssemia, but it is also one of the easiest to improve. The first thing that Kyle and Marty decided on was a way to do this. They began by writing down the plan in a notebook, which they could use not only to guide them but also to keep track of Kyle's progress. The plan included the following activities:

- Use the videotape of Kyle in a conversation to show him that his eye contact is minimal.
- Marty and Kyle converse with one another. Marty has a "clicker" or other noisemaking object in his hand, and sounds it every time Kyle looks away inappropriately or for longer than feels right.
- Sitting facing each other, Kyle practices staring down Marty, with the goal of learning to fix his eyes on someone for longer periods of time.
- Kyle watches a dog or other animal in a park and tries to keep his gaze fixed for as long as possible as the animal moves around. (We suggest staring at dogs or other animals as they move because they don't get upset when you do this. There are exceptions, however. Never stare at a dog that is staring and growling at you. The eye contact in that case is a challenge and you might get bitten!) Another way to practice this is to pick out a character in a movie and follow his or her movements (rather than be drawn to the speaking character only).
- Kyle observes the eye contact of people that he knows, especially ones who are particularly interpersonally effective.

- Kyle looks in a mirror regularly and views how he appears to others when he looks them straight in the eye. Marty uses the camcorder to show Kyle what it looks like when he is talking to someone and is not looking at his or her eyes.
- Kyle and Marty use a technique called *facial zoning* to help Kyle learn about the critical parts of other people's faces in terms of nonverbal information. As seen in the accompanying illustration, Kyle learns to focus most on zone 1 and least on zone 2.
- Since Kyle has trouble with eye contact in front of groups, he gives a mock speech or presentation. Marty sits in the audience with his clicker and clicks when Kyle loses eye contact with his audience, as represented by empty chairs. In a speech, the eye contact must move around, but should never be aimed over the heads of everyone or at their feet.

The activities we describe are strategies developed by Kyle and Marty, but you can adapt them to your own needs. Further, should you have problems in other areas in section A of the DRS, try to generate similar sorts of activities. In most cases, the camcorder will be your most effective and useful tool. Remember, research has shown that eye contact and smiling are the two most important skills present in interpersonally successful people. Work hard on your eye contact and gaze. Try to become aware of how much you are looking at people when you talk with them. Try to get as much information from them visually as possible.

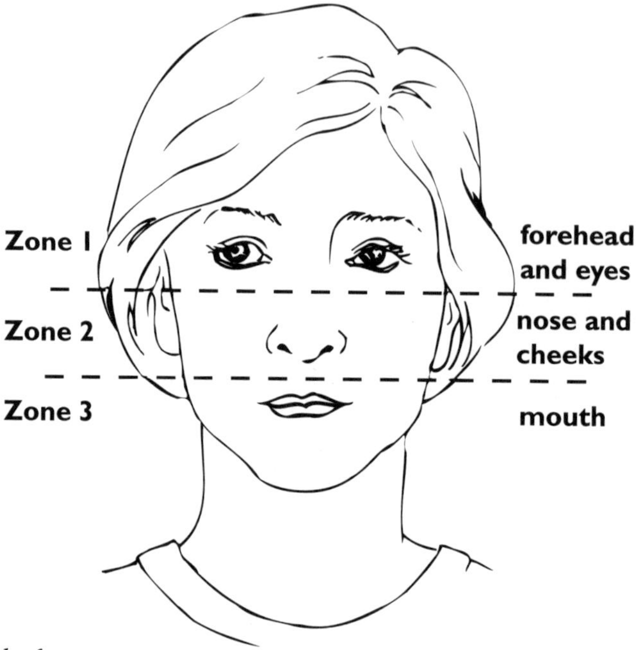

Zones of the face

Specific Approaches to Remediating Problems in Space or Touch

Based on Marty's observations, Kyle had problems in using space, but not in using touch. Given this, we'll talk about Kyle's work on space and then provide some examples of specific methods used by other people who did have problems in communicating through touch.

Focusing on Space Usage

Kyle stands too close to people when he talks with them, and tends to pull back if others get close to him. He seems not to know his own boundaries. This is a surprisingly common problem and there are several ways to fix it.

- Kyle and Marty start by learning about the four zones of personal space that we discussed earlier—intimate, personal, social, and public. They lay out a piece of masking tape on the floor with marks at eighteen inches, four feet, and twelve feet. Marty then stands at one end of the tape (the zero point) and begins to talk about various topics, some private, some public. Kyle tries to position himself appropriately on the tape to reflect the topic. For example, when Marty says, "Kyle, do you have the information on the Jones account?," Kyle should be in the personal zone, about four feet away. When Marty says, "Kyle, how is your sister feeling after the birth of her baby?," Kyle should be within the intimate zone, between zero and eighteen inches.
- Standing at the zero point on the tape on the floor, Marty describes himself as various people Kyle might encounter in an average day—a close friend, a new client, a policeman, a minister, a coworker of the same status, and an upper-level manager. Kyle starts at the far end of the tape and walks toward Marty, stopping when he comes to what he feels to be the most comfortable distance for him. Marty—and the tape—provide feedback about the spot he selected to stop.
- Marty and Kyle pick up folding chairs. Marty sets his up and sits down. Kyle then comes toward Marty and sets up his. Is he too close? Too far? Marty then adopts the roles of various people as in the exercise above. He describes varying situations. Kyle learns to adjust his chair placement accordingly.
- Kyle stands at the zero point on the tape. Marty walks toward him. Kyle says stop when he begins to feel that Marty is too close for his comfort. Marty and the tape provide Kyle with feedback about his degree of sensitivity to

people getting too close to him. Various roles are adopted by Marty as he approaches Kyle. For example, Marty says, "I'm Rosita in the office and I'm coming to ask you if you'd like to go to lunch." Or "I'm that guy on the fourth floor who always tries to tell us those terrible dirty jokes in public."

Focusing on Touch

Kyle doesn't have problems in the area of touch, so we'll give you some basic techniques that you can apply and modify on your own.

- Recall our recommendation about touching people in the United States: Don't touch anybody anywhere on their body at any time. This is sadly very close to the actual rule that we Americans live by. We are not a people who like to be touched by anyone other than friends or family, so a good rule of thumb is simply not to touch other people. In this way, you will be safe from misinterpretation or offense. Of course, the one touch that is usually welcome and required is a handshake.
- Examine the way you shake hands. Shake hands with your coach and talk about what your handshake says. Most people feel that a handshake should be firm—not too strong, but definitely not weak. Further, a good handshake is usually accompanied by good eye contact and a smile (there are the two keys again). Sometimes people use two hands in a handshake. Talk this over with your coach. When is this appropriate? Try using the left hand in different positions—e.g., cupping the back of the right hand of the other person, touching the right forearm, touching the side of the bicep, touching the shoulder. You will see that these can mean

very different things. Be sure you understand them when you use them with others and when others use them with you!

- Try to write down as many feelings as possible that you can communicate through touch. Consider the variables involved, such as where you can touch, how hard or soft, and when. Think also about people you know who touch a lot and whether it works for them or not.
- Learn the basics of touch. Be sure that you learn about the "safe" places to touch others. Generally, people will not be offended if you touch them on the outside of their arms. Never touch people's faces or hair unless you know them *very* well. Never touch people inside their arms (between their arms and torso).
- Watch carefully when people touch one another. Pay careful attention to how characters touch in movies and in advertisements, and by observing real people at malls and in office building—the streets and neighborhoods are your laboratory. See if you can learn what the rules are. Know also that touch rules vary immensely from country to country and from group to group within a culture. If you do international work or interregional work, talk about the variations in your touch behavior that it will be necessary to master. Remember Roger Axtell's book on gestures and how their meanings vary from country to country.

Specific Approaches to Remediation of Paralanguage

Paralanguage, or *how* words are said, was definitely an area of concern for Kyle, so we'll be able to describe some of the specific things he and Marty did to work on this skill. Kyle's major problem was that he did not modulate the loudness of his voice to fit the situation he was in. Here's how he and his coach remediated this.

- First, Kyle and Marty listened to and watched the tapes they had made. Marty tried to point out that Kyle did not vary his voice loudness appreciably when topics or settings changed. Most of the time, Kyle spoke as if he were in a large group, giving a speech or performing in a theater troupe. To address this deficit, Kyle read from a book (the content was secondary) while Marty called out situations such as "in front of a group of twenty-five people at a presentation," "outside an office door," "in the copy room," "in my office talking with me about a project," etc. When Marty called out a situational change, Kyle was to respond with a suitable and appropriate shift in the loudness of his voice. Marty responded immediately with feedback. Next, Marty took the book and started reading aloud. He altered his loudness without warning and Kyle noted the change and then described the appropriate topic or situation that would go along with Marty's level of speech.
- Kyle and Marty also watched one of the popular television shows about lawyers. These are especially good for working on loudness because there seems to be an astonishing amount of shouting as well as *sotto voce* conversations. They focused on loudness levels and what these communicated to the viewers, as well as their impact on the characters involved.

People other than Kyle have had problems in the other major domains of paralanguage, such as rate of speech and tone of voice. Here are a few examples of their remediation strategies in these areas.

- Start with a video- or audiotape of yourself and focus on the nonverbal pattern of the moment. Ask your coach for his or her impression. Read your own speech rate as if you were listening to someone else.

- Start to read text from a book. Read at what you feel is a normal rate. Your coach chimes in and names an emotion, such as anger, sadness, happiness, or fear. Alter the speed of your reading to match the emotion named. Additionally, the coach names situations (social conversation, presentation to a client, etc.) and you alter your speech rate accordingly. The coach provides feedback.
- Your coach reads aloud from a book and alters his or her speech rate at random times. You practice attending to the speech change and stating the possible emotional or situational bases for them. Also, watch those lawyer shows again and attend to their rate of speech. When do they speed up or slow down? What is the impact?
- Watch the tapes and focus on your tone of voice. Even if you and your coach feel that there is no problem in voice tone, you can always benefit from improving your skill there since it alone accounts for nearly 40 percent of your interpersonal impact.
- Read a book aloud. Your coach names various emotions and you alter your tone of voice accordingly. However, now the coach adds degrees of intensity to the descriptions. Thus, you will need to shift from reading in an "extremely happy" mode to an "extremely angry" mode to a "mildly sad" mode. This is hard, but very important. Stay with it. On the receptive side, your coach reads aloud and alters his or her tone within the range of intensity and types of emotion. You try to detect the change in mood and describe it.
- In an effort to focus on the interaction between emotion and situation that voice tone must accommodate, read aloud while your coach provides conditions such as "anger in a small office," "extreme happiness in a quiet restaurant," "fearfulness at a business meeting," etc. You and your coach might write these down before you start so he or she does not have to invent them on the spot.

- Now go back to the lawyer shows or the soap operas. Turn your back to the screen. This is a chance to do something called *cross-channeling.* Listen to the tone of voice of the character speaking and try to adopt the facial expression that he or she is likely to be exhibiting. As the emotions change on the show, change your facial expression accordingly. Try to do the same thing with your body posture, adopting the stance that fits the tone of voice. This is hard and most people are imperfect at it. However, it provides a good sensitizing and focusing experience for just about everyone who tries it.
- One last area of voice tone and paralanguage has to do with *disrupters* and *nonverbal vocalizations.* Recall that disrupters are words or phrases that people insert in their speech out of habit. Most people don't even know they are using them, but they can be incredibly distracting and if an employer has a choice between a prospective employee who uses these disrupters and someone else with equal skills who does not, guess which way a hiring or promotion decision will go? The most widely used disrupters vary from one generation to the next. Phrases such as "y'know," "like," and "I mean" are most common today. These are sprinkled liberally in conversations, contributing nothing to the content. Listen to a tape of yourself. Ask your coach. If you are guilty of like y'know I mean these y'know things, like I mean y'know you y'know should like stop them like y'know if you can. . . . Y'know?
- Lastly, a few words about nonverbal vocalizations. During the first Gore-Bush presidential debate in the fall of 2000, the content of both candidates' answers was rather dull and predictable. However, the commentators latched onto Gore's tendency to sigh when Bush said things he did not like. He was very strongly advised by speech coaches to stop doing that because no matter what the interpretation

of the sigh (tired, sad, frustrated, impatient), it was not so-called "presidential" behavior. Somebody was coaching Gore on his paralinguistics, because in the second debate, the sighs were gone!

There are many sounds that we make that serve little or no purpose in actual communication, but which can either greatly improve our impact on others or harm us. In the positive category might be an appreciative "Mmmmmmm" sound when someone gives us a cookie they baked. On the negative side, and in the same class as the inappropriate sigh, would be unconscious snorting, sniffing, throat-clearing, lip-smacking, and other sounds that people can find grating. Don't get us wrong, the well-placed "raspberry" sound, for instance, can say much more than the words, "I really don't like the way you Atlanta Braves are playing today." However, this very power of the nonverbal vocalization argues for its very judicious use.

Specific Approaches to the Remediation of Facial Expression

Marty and Kyle really had just one major area of concern with regard to facial expressions, and it was an expressive one. Kyle was hard to read. No matter if the topic was one that was emotional and interesting or bland and boring, Kyle's face remained a blank slate. This problem was addressed as follows:

- Using the reading-aloud procedure, Marty sat with Kyle and called out various emotions. Kyle then tried to produce a facial expression *and* voice tone that matched that emotion. Marty provided feedback about Kyle's performance.
- Using a digital camera, Marty took some photos of Kyle. Marty announced an emotion and Kyle tried to produce the facial expression that went with it. They then examined the

photo together. They repeated this procedure until Kyle was able to reliably produce a very clear facial expression depicting all basic emotions. Kyle focused on how his face felt when his facial expression was just right. The feedback from the photos was essential.

- Marty and Kyle worked on Kyle's resting face. Marty took photos of Kyle when he was working on something other than facial expressions. A good time for this is when Kyle was either writing and concentrating or while he was waiting for something—like a tape recording or video—to start. They examined the resting face. Again Kyle worked on developing a less blank and slightly positive resting face.
- In addition to his work with Marty, we also urged Kyle to work alone with a mirror at home. Many people we talk with who are very effective interpersonally have practiced at a mirror. They learned what different emotional expressions looked like. Using a mirror in this way gives us a chance for a personal Robert Burns Moment.

Kyle's problems in facial expression were primarily expressive. Here are some techniques for remediating receptive skills in reading facial expressions. As usual, try to adapt the suggestions to your own needs.

- Sit in front of a mirror with your coach next to you. When your coach makes a particular facial expression, first name it, then try to mimic it. Then reverse roles: You produce a facial expression and see if your coach sees it the way you intended.
- Start with looking at paintings and identifying peak-still facial expressions. Then move to photos from magazines and photos of people whom you might know. Identify the emotions. What is the feeling? How intense is it? Now move to

the more dynamic characters on TV. Choose a variety of show types, from news to dramas and comedies. Finally, take a trip to the mall. Sit and watch people with your coach. Describe the feelings that you see. Attend especially to resting faces. Try to guess the content of the interactions among people based solely on their facial expressions.

- Do some behavioral borrowing. Find some people you know who have particularly clear facial expressions and see if you can borrow them. *Be sure that you and your coach agree on the facial expressions you choose!*
- Incorporate context into interpretation of faces in a systematic way. Use photos or paintings. Examine the context in which facial expressions occur. Could you guess the emotions from just the context? Imagine how a facial expression's meaning would change if the context were different. For example, if you are looking at an angry face, try to describe a context in which the facial expression might be interpreted otherwise.

Specific Remediation Approaches to Problems with Fashion (Objectics)

Since we have no specific example from Kyle to help us focus on fashion cues, we'll describe some remediation methods here as they were developed for a young assistant office manager named Michael. Michael's problem was in expressive objectics; his office and desk tended to be in total disarray. While this might work well for one of us college professors, in an accounting office of a large city government, it definitely did not work!

- Michael's coach was a senior supervisor named Donald. As he started to observe Michael, he quickly realized that

Michael's messiness at work was probably not work-specific. He looked in Michael's car. Empty coffee cups and soda cans were strewn on the back seat. While Michael did not necessarily need to clean up his entire life (so to speak), something had to be done at his office. His absence of order communicated something about him that was not positive because he was in charge of keeping things organized. To increase Michael's awareness, Donald took him to visit other offices. They talked about what each office communicated about its occupant.

- Many people do not know how to dress for success. This does not mean that they do not know exactly what outfits to wear according to fashion dictates. What they do not realize is the degree to which clothing and style of dress in general are a major channel of nonverbal communication. Just as they would not use street lingo in a business meeting, Michael needed to learn that he could not use home or car standards in his office. In chapter 5 we mentioned Molloy's book *Dress for Success.* It is an excellent resource to help people who want to improve the message they send through their clothing.
- To increase awareness of objectics, spend some time either with your coach or alone focusing only on the style of dress of people you know as well as people you see on the street, in the malls, on airplanes, etc. Try to understand what they are saying with their clothes. Most people, by the way, do not put on an item of clothing and think to themselves, "This says bold and arrogant!" In fact, most people put on things that are comfortable for them, but that comfort is related to the degree to which they feel that how they look matches with the interpersonal requirements that they read in situations.
- Try this exercise. Catalog all of the objectic items that you use. Include clothing and accessories, but also items such as

perfumes and aftershave lotions, the objects you carry (briefcases, bags, purses), the way your home is furnished, and the kind of car that you drive. With the help of your coach, examine your objectic messages to others based on these items. Once you have learned that the Hawaiian shirt makes you look like a throwback to *Gilligan's Island*, do you still want to wear it? Try to compose the ideal objective presentation for you. You will, we are very sure, be most uncomfortable at first with the idea of adopting it. The important thing is to see your pattern of fashion cues as one of the choices that you make, and that you tune it to your situation, stage of development, and moment-to-moment needs. Of course, most of us have limits on our ability to implement any ideal presentation. The important thing is to try as hard as we can to achieve our ideal and to know that variation is possible and desirable.

Specific Remediation Techniques for Expressive and Receptive Use of the Hands

One of the best ways to supplement our knowledge of social and other interpersonal situations is through increased awareness of the hands. Surprisingly, however, people—even people who are very good at nonverbal communication—tend to pay the least amount of attention to what hands can tell us. Therefore, almost anyone can benefit from the exercises we have developed for expressive and receptive communication using the hands.

- Information about receptive communication with the hands is all around us, but we suggest that you start by examining either paintings or photos. Use the technique that we described in chapter 7, where you cover the faces of the people you are looking at and pay specific attention to their hands. With or without your coach, try to learn as much as possible about the situation and the feelings for the characters by using *only* the hands. If you are like most people, this will be a very exciting discovery. There is an immense amount communicated, even in these still pictures.

- Having practiced with peak stills and photos, turn to the more dynamic avenues, TV and movies. Again, cover over the faces and upper bodies. (Remember, do this simply by placing your index finger across your visual field in such a way that it serves as a block. This immediately makes the hand positions and gestures "louder.") The power of hands to communicate was brought home to us through a TV lawyer show we saw during the writing of this chapter. Instead of the usual focus on the faces of all those involved, the verdict was delivered while the camera focused only on the hands of the various characters. It isolated the hands of some anxious adoptive parents, on the hands of the birth mother, on the two attorneys. We were struck by three things: how clearly the hands communicated the feelings of the characters; the incredible intensity of the now-familiar verdict scene depicted in this way; and the insight of the director. Expose yourself to similar experiences. See how much is out there that usually goes unnoticed.
- Now shift to real live interactions. Start looking at the hands of the people you are with. This is easier, of course, if you are in a meeting where other people are talking and you can observe their hand positions and gestures without looking like you're ignoring your responsibility in a face-to-face interaction. See how the movements or positions of people's hands tell you so much—the person who appears calm, but is fidgeting with his hand or rings; the person who is talking tough but whose hand position betrays a weak resolve. We believe that whether we attend to these cues or not, they affect us and determine much of our responses to

others. You can get a major edge on all of your interactions if you read people's hands well.

- On the expressive side, you now realize that you are giving off as much information in your own hands as you can get from others. Examine the videotapes of yourself. Look at photos of yourself in various situations. How do your hands look? What do they say? What do you want them to say? Practice increasing your awareness of your hand positions. Find a good resting hand position and use it often. During your social and business interactions, try to attend to your hands now and then. This can be very hard to do. The position of our hands seems rapidly to slip out of awareness. Perhaps that is why it leaks so much about us, and why we can trust the information gained there so strongly.

Specific Techniques for Problems in Gestures and Postures

Many hand positions have become so familiar that they have evolved into purposeful gestures that communicate what we intend. Often, however, we are unaware of the other ways in which we use our hands and arms to communicate. Most common among these are pounding a table for emphasis or pointing at something or someone in order to get or direct their attention.

Expressive problems in gestural communication typically arise when gestures are not used at all or sufficiently frequently, rendering our nonverbal interactions rather dull; when gestures are too big or too loud, thereby distracting others from the content of our verbal messages; and when our gestures are unknowingly (and sometimes knowingly) offensive. On the receptive side, gestural dyssemia is most typically observed when people either do not know the meanings of gestures they see or when their eye contact is so poor that they simply miss the gestural components in their conversations.

- Because they operate through the visual channel, expressive gestural problems are most effectively remediated via videotaping. Using the video that you and your coach prepared during the assessment process, examine your gestures carefully. Are they clear? Are they properly timed? Does the intensity of your gestures match the intensity of your feeling?
- Focus on the gestures used by your friends and coworkers. Are there any that you do not fully comprehend? Talk with your coach about them. Learn what they mean. Do you notice any gestural patterns that you and your coach find particularly appealing or effective? Try to borrow them. Watch the gestural patterns of people who have succeeded in your career area. Observe the gestures and postures of people who are successful socially. Ask your coach to give you a reading on the degree to which your gestures and postures say what you want them to say.
- Through use of your videos and photos, examine your resting posture. Determine whether your posture actually says what you want to say. If it does not, experiment with other postures and seek feedback from your coach. Attend to the ways in which others around you vary their postures according to the situation they are in. What seems to be the ideal business meeting posture? What is the best posture when talking to a person you are interested in socially? Every posture is a word in your nonverbal vocabulary. Choose postures and use them as carefully as you would any other word. If a situation is one where you would think carefully about what you say verbally (like a job interview), chances are that this is also a situation in which you should watch what you say nonverbally.
- Make it a practice to observe people's gestures and postures in the magazines you read and the movies you see. You will be quickly amazed at how much advertising agencies take advantage of nonverbal language that is normally out of our

awareness. You will be impressed, as we are, by their sophistication in knowing which images will produce the desired reactions. Try to understand how advertisements use postures, gestures, and facial expressions to say what they want to say without using words.

- Experiment with sitting, standing, and walking postures. Each is important in its own right. Ask your coach to give you feedback on how you sit, how you stand, and how you walk. What are you telling others in each of these?

Specific Remediation Approaches for Deficits in Awareness of Social Norms

To this point, most of the remediation work we've been describing has dealt with behavioral rules that are not formally written down anywhere—the residual rules that were only noticed when they are broken (see the introduction). Many social norms are also unwritten, but there are also many we need to follow that have actually been committed to paper in etiquette, relationship, and vocational books. For decades, Emily Post's book *Etiquette* was the prime source for these written social rules, but it has now been joined by the writings of Judith Martin, whom most of us know as "Miss Manners." To be sure, anyone who needs to answer invitations, learn which fork to use when, get lessons on the proper way to introduce people, and such can and ought simply turn to these books on etiquette—in these hurried times, we all could probably benefit from perusing them. While we would not go so far as to say that someone lacking in the knowledge of social graces is dyssemic, the absence of knowledge of etiquette can certainly hamper one's progress towards social and vocational success.

In addition to the written social norms, however, there are also many unwritten norms and rules that people must know if they are to be capable of smooth and effective interactions and successful relationships. While many of these unwritten rules are universal, many others vary from culture to culture and from one era to another. They also can vary from one type of business to another and from one office to another. They must be learned. Marty noticed that Kyle had not learned them well.

- Kyle sometimes seemed tactless. He said things that were better left unsaid. He sometimes insulted people or hurt their feelings without meaning to. To help him remedy this, Marty needed to observe Kyle closely to identify some examples of his tactlessness. Kyle also increased his awareness of this problem by asking two coworkers if he had ever said anything to them that seemed tactless or unfeeling. He prefaced this request by stating that he had been concerned about being tactless and that he was on a self-improvement campaign. In this way, he found that when he responded to an invitation for lunch with Rosita by saying loudly, "I hate Mexican food," that he had embarrassed her. A simple "Thanks, no, I think I'll eat here today," would have sufficed.
- Marty talked with Kyle about how office doors were used to indicate people's availability. He showed him—and Kyle had been totally unaware of this—how the degree to which the door was open said whether or not the person could be interrupted. Wide open meant come in. Half open meant "I'm busy, but if it's important, knock." Just open, but not closed, meant, "You can interrupt me if it's really, really important, but knock first." Finally, a closed door meant "Go away." Marty and Kyle went over a number of other signal systems in the office. They talked about how long it was permissible to schmooze in the hall. They talked about what sorts of topics were okay at the water cooler or in the coffee room. While Kyle knew some of these rules already, the discussion sensitized him to the sorts of things that he needed to look

for. Further, from then on, he knew how to use *his* office door to signal people about his own availability.

- Marty also talked to Kyle about his ill-fated efforts to make witty remarks. He explained that while most people understood he was trying to be funny or sound smart, his comments usually missed their mark. Rather than put Kyle through a crash course in comic delivery, Marty suggested that Kyle should simply be more straightforward. He and Marty practiced responding differently to some situations in which Kyle remembered feeling badly after an errant remark. One example was the interaction he had written about in his diary involving his fellow church congregant in the supermarket.
- If your coach suggests that you have problems using etiquette or navigating social norms, take him or her very seriously. We know from experience that small errors can have incredibly great impact in this domain. Try to attend to the things other people do that bother you a little, a moderate amount, or a great deal. Try the following classic exercise:

1. Write down a list of sentences structured as follows: "Everything would be fine between__________and me if only he (she) would__________"

2. Make the list as long as you would like and include as many people as you can. Once the list is done, read it aloud but replace the third-person pronouns (he, she, her, his, them, their) with first-person pronouns (I, me, my, mine). Let's say you wrote, "Everything would be fine between Marty and me if only he would pay more attention to me when I talk." When you read the sentence aloud, it would say, "Everything would be fine between Marty and me if only *I* would pay more attention to *him* when *he* talks." Try this and think about whether you are in fact guilty of the very

same things you are bothered by in others. You will be surprised at how much you learn from this exercise. Work on what you learn from it.

Specific Techniques for Improving Conversational Skills

You probably have noticed that there are some people who can talk with anyone about anything at any time. To be sure, extremely eusemic people are unusual, but we all know some of them. However, you also likely know some people who *desperately* need to be aware of and remediate their conversational skills. A business executive friend of ours told us of an incident on an airplane wherein he was accosted by a well-meaning young man who talked to him for "every single second of a two-and-a-half-hour flight and never ever said anything worth hearing." The executive said that he did everything he could to give the young man hints that he was busy and would prefer not to talk, but all hints went unheeded. This young man certainly did not mean to alienate the executive. In fact, he probably thought he was making a new business contact. He was very wrong.

Improving your conversational skills can be done in two phases. First, you must observe others in conversation and apply what you've learned about nonverbal language. Watch the conversationalists' body postures, their gestures. Do they lean forward? Do they tend to mirror one another's postures? (This is often a sign of two people who have connected.) How about their tone of voice? Eye contact? As we said, everything comes together in this real interaction. Watch yourself in a conversation via videotape. How do you look? Like the good conversationalists? If not, what behaviors might you borrow from them?

- Nothing beats having actual conversations with a variety of people in a variety of situations. Try not to demand perfection of yourself. You will make many a blunder on your way to improved conversational skills. Start out by role-playing with your coach. Imagine that he or she is a peer, a superior, a customer, whatever you choose. Think about the way you say your words. Attend to the signals that set the pace for the conversation. Watch for the "voice drop" at the end of the other person's comment; this usually means it's your turn. Watch for the tonal emphasis that can mean the same thing. Watch for the other person's eyes fixing on you as he or she comes to the end of a comment. Never step on the closing words of other people's sentences (even though you, like most people, already know what the final words are likely to be). Extend people the courtesy of finishing their thoughts. If you ever hear people say to you something akin to, "Let me finish my point," you have likely interrupted them and need to step back.

- Conversations are like symphonies. They have beginnings, middles, and ends. At the beginning there is some basic introductory material that must be experienced before plunging into the heart of the piece. As the music draws to a close there are also definite signs that we can pick up. Meetings are like this as well. Practice judging when a meeting has gotten past its beginning point; try to judge when the meeting has started to end. Do this with conversations. Try to learn the cues (there are lots of them) that you can use to determine when the opening has ended and it is time to get to the topic at hand. Try to know when the conversation is getting near its end. We imagine you know some people who cannot end a conversation well. They stay on the phone too long. They linger as they leave parties or other events. We are reminded here of a classic skit on *Saturday Night Live* where John Belushi portrayed "the thing that would not leave." Despite such strong hints as the host and hostess putting on pajamas and turning out the lights, the Belushi character went on talking. What is very funny on TV can be excruciatingly difficult in real life. Learn the cues to conversational timing and follow them.

- As important as conversational timing, the last area that must be mastered is choice of conversational topics. It is obvious that the topics of conversations must fit the situation in which they occur. Office conversations rarely have room for intimacies and intimate conversations over dinner that focus only on the office are doomed to failure. Further, to be a good conversationalist, you must be able to discuss a variety of topics. Such knowledge is readily available through reading news magazines, newspapers, or books, by watching TV, by developing hobbies, and by pursuing a passion.
- There is one topic, however, that is always at the ready and that is capitalized on by really skilled conversationalists. That topic is the life, interests, and experiences of the person to whom you are talking. We have known people who could talk with other people for hours and never say anything about themselves, skillfully directing the conversation to information about the other person. We all love to talk about ourselves and if people ask us to do this, we tend to enjoy talking with them without really knowing why. Watch Barbara Walters or other skilled interviewers. They say almost nothing about themselves, yet their conversations seem very interesting and lively. Learn how to ask other people about themselves. Be interested in them with all of your nonverbal and verbal skills. Your conversations will take a leap forward.

Specific Methods for the Remediation of Problems in Chronemics and Time Usage

As you remember from chapter 3, our general rhythm or pace of living and the way we use time are both important sources of nonverbal information about us. Though seemingly a small thing to many people, being made to wait for others who are habitually late can be really bothersome. Businesspeople who are kept waiting can be more than bothered; they can refuse to do business with you. To be sure, poor use of time can be very costly to you. Remediation techniques in chronemics and time usage fall into two main categories: those directed at becoming aware of our (and other people's) rhythms and those directed at simple punctuality and respect for other people's schedules.

- In general, the higher the status of people or the more we hope to benefit from their meeting with us, the longer we should be willing to wait. Conversely, the higher ranking or more important the other person, the less time he or she should be made to wait for us. People will wait many hours for a very late president of the United States, but the president is not likely to wait more than a few seconds for one of us. Most of us will wait more than an hour, usually without complaining, if we are going to see a physician; however, if the doctor comes to the waiting room and we are not there, he or she will move on to the next name on the list!
- Become aware of the time requirements in your office. With your coach, generate a list of the people with whom you might interact. Rank-order them from top to bottom. Learn how long you should wait for them. Know which ones should wait for you. Know which ones you should *never* keep waiting. Hint: Never keep your boss or someone you are trying to impress socially waiting.
- Keep a diary of your appointments and meetings. Note how many minutes early or late you were for each. Identify your pattern. If you are always late, try to find some ways to adjust your leaving time so that you can arrive on time. We have found that many people are late for things because they cannot estimate accurately how long it will take them

to get to their destination. If this is a chronic problem for you, practice with your coach judging how long it should take to get from your office to your boss's office or how long it should take you from a meeting downtown to one uptown. Travel-time estimation is a skill that can be learned, although it takes some effort.

- Learn a skill that we call *rhythm matching.* We know that wherever they come from, people tend to feel strangely comfortable with people from their home area. This is generally because they think, move, eat, and talk at about the same pace. With your coach, practice adjusting your speaking rate as he or she varies it. When you eat dinner with people, try to finish your food at about the same time they do. We knew a businessman who had discovered this on his own and told us about it. No matter where he was in the world, his dinner meetings were always successful because people always felt comfortable with him—never too rushed, never too slow. To slow down, put your fork down, eat smaller bites; you can make a meal last a long time (by American standards) if you practice.
- You can also match the pace at which you walk with people. A group of people tends to walk at a speed set by some mysterious force—sometimes one of its members, sometimes by its purpose or the situation. Observe whether you fall behind or move ahead. Try to match your rhythm to that of the group. If you are with another person, be aware of the status differential between you. If you are with a superior, match his or her pace. If you are with a subordinate, be aware that he or she is most likely keying off of you.
- The United States is a monochronic time country. We think of time as a commodity that we either can sell to people or give to them. When you agree to work for a salary, you sell your time to people. When they get your time in return for

money, they feel that they own it and expect to use it for their own purposes. When you give your time without recompense, however, you are saying something very special: that you are willing to go beyond what is expected and give something of yourself without asking for something in return. This is why people who voluntarily put in overtime at their place of work are often seen as better employees, as go-getters, as people interested in moving up. While there is nothing wrong with leaving work on time on an ordinary day, one can communicate much to one's employers or friends by simply staying longer to do something that needs doing despite the workday's having ended.

Giving of your time is indeed equivalent to giving of yourself, and people appreciate this immensely. With your coach, think of some opportunities where you can give your time freely in order to communicate your commitment to other people. The effect is just as strong in a social relationship where, for example, going out of your way (using your time) to save another person some effort or time is received most appreciatively.

Some Final Thoughts as We End with You

In this chapter, we have provided you with two essentials. First, of course, are the examples of specific remediation activities that you can adapt to your own needs. Second, however, is a broad sense of how remediation methods are generated. Remediation follows from assessment. There is no one standardized way of helping each and every one of you become more skilled nonverbally and interpersonally. Your own specific remediation will follow from your own specific assessment. In honing your skills, we counsel patience. It takes a long time to develop interpersonal skills—to move from the dyssemic side of the nonverbal skill dimension to the eusemic side of things, where interpersonal interactions are smoother and more successful.

Here are some reminders regarding your expectations for overcoming dyssemia. First, remember that if you have good receptive skills and your problems are in the expressive domain, you are in a fortunate position. Our research and clinical experience have shown that if people with good receptive skills can simply focus on their own nonverbal behavior—with such helps as audiotapes, videotapes, photographs, and mirrors—they can recognize their problem areas and work on them relatively rapidly. (The "relatively" here is compared with the time needed to overcome *both* expressive and receptive problems or receptive problems alone.)

We have also found that there is a association between which nonverbal channels are dyssemic and the amount of time needed for remediation. Fashion difficulties can be fixed relatively quickly because they don't require continuous attention. The same is true for skills in the use of time, such as being on time for meetings or appointments. Facial expressions and space problems may take a bit more time. Still more time must be set aside for less commonly watched behaviors such as postures, hand positions, gestures, and touch. Probably the most time required would be for the diffuse, foundational areas like rhythm, conversational skills, and social norms.

These are simply rough estimates. We have known some people who have overcome immense problems in a very short time and we have known others who have required more time and practice to remediate a simple problem in eye contact. The take-home message is this and, believe it or not, we first saw it written on the back of a T-shirt: There are no shortcuts to anywhere worth going. The journey from dyssemia to eusemia will take time. It will take effort. But when you finally arrive, you and those around you will be very happy that you made the trip.

Bon voyage!

Appendix A

Locus of Control Scale for Adults

We are trying to find out what men and women think about certain things. We want you to answer the following questions the way you feel. Different people will answer in different ways. Don't take too much time answering any one question, but do try to answer them all, and try to pick one or the other response for all the questions and not leave any blank.

One of your concerns during the test may be, "What should I do if I can answer both yes and no to a question?" It's not unusual for that to happen. If it does, think about whether your answer is just a little more one way than the other. For example, if you'd assign a weighting of 51 percent to "yes" 49 percent to "no," then make your answer "yes."

__Y__ 1. Do you believe that most problems will solve themselves if you just don't fool with them?

__N__ 2. Do you believe that you can stop yourself from catching a cold?

__Y__ 3. Are some people just born lucky?

__N__ 4. In school, did you feel most of the time that getting good grades meant a great deal to you?

__Y__ 5. Are you often blamed for things that aren't your fault?

__N__ 6. Do you believe that if somebody studies hard enough he or she can pass any subject?

__Y__ 7. Do you feel that most of the time it doesn't pay to try hard because things never turn out right anyway?

__Y__ 8. Do you feel that if things start out well in the morning it's going to be a good day, no matter what you do?

__N__ 9. Do you feel that most of the time parents listen to what their children have to say?

__Y__ 10. Do you believe that wishing can make good things happen?

__Y__ 11. When you get reprimanded, does it usually seem it's for no good reason at all?

__Y__ 12. Most of the time do you find it hard to change a friend's opinion?

__N__ 13. Do you think that cheering more than luck helps a team to win?

__Y__ 14. Did you feel that it was nearly impossible to change your parents' minds about anything?

__N__ 15. Do you believe that parents should allow children to make most of their own decisions?

__Y__ 16. Do you feel that when you do something wrong there's very little you can do to make it right?

__Y__ 17. Do you believe that most people who are good at sports are just born that way?

__Y__ 18. Are most of the other people your age stronger than you are?

__Y__ 19. Do you feel that one of the best ways to handle most problems is just not to think about them?

__N__ 20. Do you feel that you have a lot of choice in deciding who your friends are?

__Y__ 21. If you find a four-leaf clover, do you believe that it might bring you good luck?

__N__ 22. Did you often feel that whether or not you did your homework had much to do with what kind of grades you got?

__Y__ 23. Do you feel that when a person is angry with you, there's little you can do to stop him or her?

__Y__ 24. Have you ever had a good-luck charm?

__N__ 25. Do you believe that whether or not people like you depends on how you act?

__N__ 26. Did your parents usually help you if you asked them to?

__Y__ 27. Have you felt that when people were angry with you it was usually for no good reason at all?

__N__ 28. Most of the time, do you feel that you can change what might happen tomorrow by what you do today?

__Y__ 29. Do you believe that when bad things are going to happen they are just going to happen, no matter what you try to do to stop them?

__N__ 30. Do you think that people can get their own way if they just keep trying?

__Y__ 31. Most of the time, did you find it useless to try and get your own way at home?

__N__ 32. Do you feel that when good things happen they happen because of hard work?

__Y__ 33. Do you feel that when somebody wants to be your enemy there's little you can do to change matters?

__N__ 34. Do you feel that it's easy to get friends to do what you want them to do?

__Y__ 35. Do you usually feel that you have little to say about what you get to eat at home?

__Y__ 36. Do you feel that when someone doesn't like you there's little you can do about it?

__Y__ 37. Did you usually feel that it was almost useless to try in school because most other children were just plain smarter than you were?

__N__ 38. Are you the kind of person who believes that planning ahead makes things turn out better?

__Y__ 39. Most of the time, do you feel that you have little to say about what your family decides to do?

__N__ 40. Do you think it's better to be smart than to be lucky?

Scoring the Scale

Give yourself one point each time your answer agrees with the keyed answer. Your score is the total number of agreements between your answers and the ones on the key. The higher the score, the more external you are.

Appendix B

Touch Observation Form

Name______________________________ Date______________

Use arrows to link entries which are part of the same interaction

Example: 1
↓
2

Indicate where applicable

BM — Best Male Friend

BF — Best Female Friend

MO — Mother

FA — Father

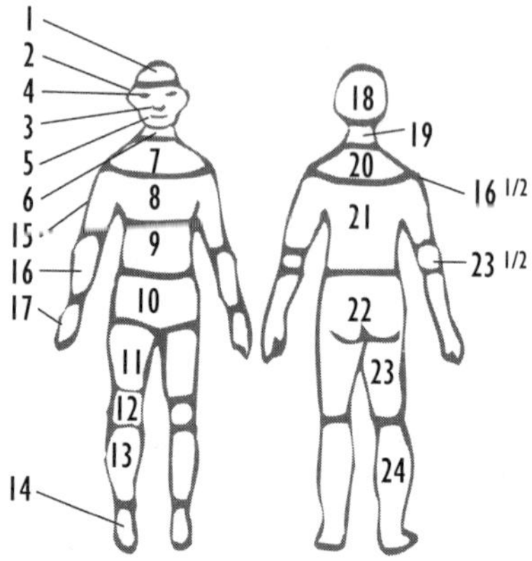

1 Initiator of touch A Me B Other C Mutual D Unclear (1 letter)	2a Parts of body when initiated (1 or more letters @ blank note 2 handed touches)		2b Parts of body when mutual or unclear (1 or more letters per blank) Me	Other	3 Place A Mine B Other's C Neutral Specify bldg. and room	4 Time of day (include a.m. or p.m.)
1________	______	______	______	______	______	______
2________	______	______	______	______	______	______
3________	______	______	______	______	______	______

5 *Accompanying verbal statement* (Paraphrase if necessary) When A immediately prior to touch B Immediately after touch C During *By* (**M**) me (**O**) other	6 *Touch translated into verbal statement* (Make into short sentence if possible. Note voice tone or facial expression if critical to meaning)	7 (Mark "Psych" for touches you reject internally only) *Acceptance / Rejection* A Touch accepted by me B Touch rejected by me C Touch accepted by Other D Touch rejected by Other (Spec with letter, explain how & why touch is rejected)
1________________	________________	________________
2________________	________________	________________
3________________	________________	________________

8
Type of touch

A Caressing/holding
B Feeling/caressing
C Prolonged holding
D Holding/pressing ag.
E Spot touching
F Accidental brushing
G handshake
H Pat/squeeze
J Punch
K Pinch
L Other
(1 or more letters)

1__________
2__________
3__________

9
Purpose of Participants

A Give/get into (specify)
B Ask/give favor
C Persuading
D Persuaded
E Casual talk
F Deeptalk
G Greeting
H Departing
I Any other (specify)

Me _____ *Other* _____

10
Others present

(Male &/or female)
(Specify relation to you using letters from Category 11)

11
Relationship to other

A. Relative (specify)
B1 Close friend
B2 Not close
C Acquaintance
D Co-worker
E Superior
F Subordinate
G Stranger
H Other (specify)
Specify if intimate

12
Nature of social occassion

A Work
B Class
C Party
D Informal meeting
E Other (specify)
For public places specify function (bar, etc.)

1__________
2__________
3__________

13
Status of other

A Higher — 1 Formal
B Lower — 2 Informal
C Equal
(1 letter and 1 No)

14
Age of other
(Approximate)

15
Sex of other
(M/F)

16
Race of other

A Anglo
B Black
C Chicano
D Asian
E Other (specify)

17
Standing or sitting

Me — Other
1_____ _____
2_____ _____
3_____ _____

18
Any other contextual factors you think influenced your touches:

____
____
____

Touch Observation Form
Used with the permission of Stanley E. Jones

Bibliography

Adler, R., and N. Towne. *Looking Out/Looking In* (San Francisco: Rinehart Press, 1975), 82.

Allen, W. *Getting Even* (New York: Random House, 1978).

Axtell, R. E. *Gestures: Do's and Taboos of Body Language around the World* (New York: John Wiley & Sons, Inc., 1998).

Birdwhistell, R. L. *Kinesics and Context* (Philadelphia: University of Pennsylvania Press, 1970).

Chapman, A. H. *Harry Stack Sullivan: His Life and His Work* (New York: G. P. Putnam's Sons, 1976).

Crusco, A. H., and C. G. Wetzel. "The Midas Touch: The Effects of Interpersonal Touching on Restaurant Tipping." *Personality and Social Psychology Bulletin* 10 (1984): 512–517.

Duke, M. P., S. Nowicki, Jr., and E. Walker. *Teaching Your Child the Language of Social Success* (Atlanta, GA: Peachtree Press, 1996).

Ekman, P., and M. O'Sullivan. "Facial Expression: Methods, Means and Monues." In S. Feldman & B. Rime (Eds.), *Fundamentals of Nonverbal Behavior* (New York: Cambridge University Press, 1991), 163–199.

Hall, E. T. *The Hidden Dimension* (New York: Doubleday, 1966).

Hall, E. T., and M. R. Hall. *Understanding Cultural Differences: Germans, French, and Americans* (New York: Intercultural Press, 1990).

Heslin, R. "Steps Toward a Taxonomy of Touching." (Paper presented to the Midwestern Psychological Association, Chicago, IL, 1974.)

Jones, S. E. "Communicating with Touch." In L. K. Guerrero, J. A. DeVito, and M. L. Hecht (Eds.), *The Nonverbal Communication Reader* (Prospect Heights, IL: Waveland Press, Inc., 1999), 192–201.

Jones, S. E., and K. Yarbough. "A Naturalistic Study of the Meanings of Touch." *Communication Monograph* 52, (1985), 19–56.

Levinson, D. J. "A Conception of Adult Development." *American Psychologist* 41, (1986), 3–14.

Levinson, D. J. *Seasons of a Woman's Life.* (New York: Knopf, 1989).

Love, E. B., M. P. Duke, and S. Nowicki, Jr. "The Emory Dyssemia Index: A Brief Screening Instrument for the Identification of Nonverbal Language Deficits in Elementary School Children." *The Journal of Psychology* 128, (1994), 703–704.

Luft, J. *Of Human Interaction* (Palo Alto: National Press, 1969).

Malloy, J. *The New Dress for Success Handbook* (New York: Warner Books, 1988).

Maysonave, S. *Casual Power: How to Power Up Your Nonverbal Communication and Dress Down for Success* (New York: Bright Books, 1999).

Morris, D. *Intimate Behaviour* (New York: Random House, 1971).

Morris, D. *Manwatching: A Field Guide to Human Behavior* (New York: Abrams, 1977).

Nowicki, S. Jr. *A Manual and Reference List for the Adult Nowicki-Strickland Locus of Control Scale.* Unpublished manuscript, Department of Psychology, Emory University, Atlanta, GA.

Nowicki, S. Jr., and M. P. Duke. "A Locus of Control Scale for College as well as Noncollege Adults." *Journal of Personality Assessment* 38 (1974), 136–137.

Nowicki, S. Jr., and M. P. Duke. *Helping the Child Who Doesn't Fit In* (Atlanta, GA: Peachtree Press, 1992).

Pei, M. Cited by R. Axtell (1998).

Rotter, J. B. "Generalized Expectancies for Internal versus External Control of Reinforcement." *Psychological Monographs* 80 (1966) (Whole No. 609).

Semic, B. "Vocal Attractiveness: What Sounds Beautiful Is Good." In L. K. Guerrero, J. A. DeVito, and M. L. Hecht (Eds.), *The Nonverbal Communication Reader* (Prospect Heights, IL: Waveland Press, Inc., 1999), 149–155.

Von Raffler-Engel, W. "Developmental Kinesics." In B. Hoffer and R. St.

Clair (Eds.), *Developmental Kinesics: The Emerging Paradigm* (Baltimore: University Park Press, 1981).

Watzlawick, P., J. H. Beavin, and D. D. Jackson. *Pragmatics of Human Communication* (New York: Norton, 1967).

Whorf, B. *Language, Thought, and Reality: Selected Writings of Benjamin Whorf.* Ed. J. B. Carroll (Cambridge, MA: Technology Press of MIT, 1956).

Index